N

WE ARE FEMINIST

An Infographic History
of the Women's
Rights Movement

Fem·in·ism

/ˈfɛmɪnɪz(ə)m/ 🔊

The advocacy of women's rights on the grounds of the equality of the sexes.

Origin: Late 19th century, from French féminisme. Coined by French philosopher and utopian socialist Charles Fourier in 1837 to mean advocacy of the rights and equality of women.

WE ARE FEMINIST

An Infographic History of the Women's Rights Movement

CONTENTS

Foreword by Helen Pankhurst **6**

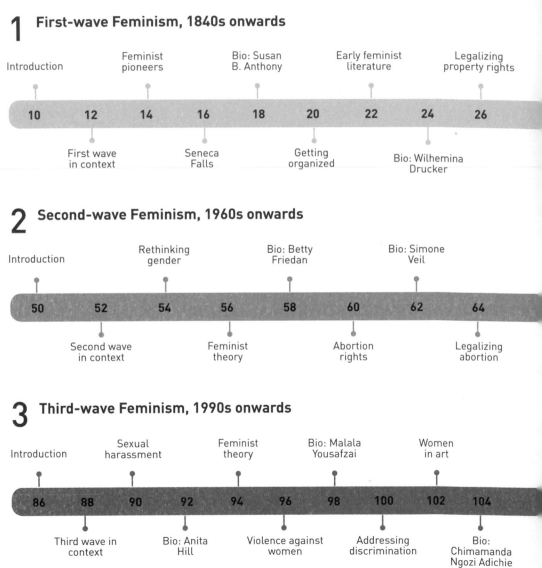

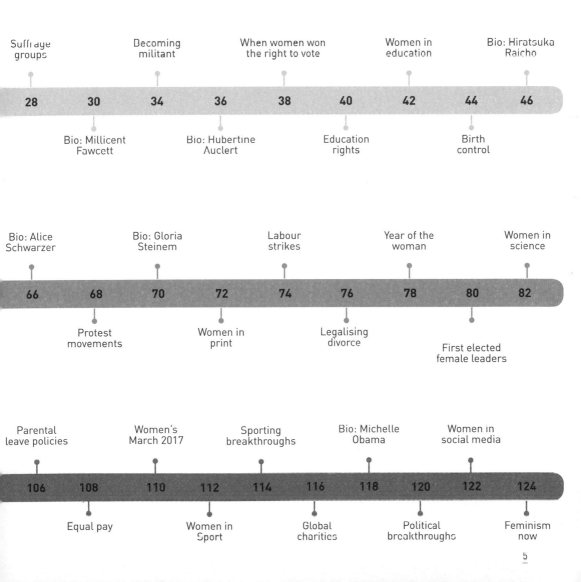

Suffrage groups

28

30 — Bio: Millicent Fawcett

Becoming militant

34

36 — Bio: Hubertine Auclert

When women won the right to vote

38

40 — Education rights

Women in education

42

44 — Birth control

Bio: Hiratsuka Raicho

46

Bio: Alice Schwarzer

66

68 — Protest movements

Bio: Gloria Steinem

70

72 — Women in print

Labour strikes

74

76 — Legalising divorce

Year of the woman

78

80 — First elected female leaders

Women in science

82

Parental leave policies

106

108 — Equal pay

Women's March 2017

110

112 — Women in Sport

Sporting breakthroughs

114

116 — Global charities

Bio: Michelle Obama

118

120 — Political breakthroughs

Women in social media

122

124 — Feminism now

We are feminist: together we stand

We are feminist. Three words, three powerful words. They remind me of three words from the suffragette struggle: 'Votes for Women', 'Deeds not Words'. Just three words that encapsulated so much activism and defiance against the status quo.

Together we stand. The words also echo the words of Faiza Vaid speaking at a march in London ahead of International Women's Day in 2017. She said 'either we fight for all, or we all fall'.

On that day, around 10,000 people stood together. This book embodies the spirit of that march... and so many other marches, and other forms of resistance through the ages. It calls to mind a speech of my great-grandmother, Emmeline Pankhurst, who declared 'Now I ask you, is there any limit to what we can do, except the limit we put on ourselves?' But the book is also portable, transportable, 'regeneratable'. It can travel to any house in any corner of the world; it can be a companion in a journey of discovery for young people everywhere.

This book is a simple and easily accessible summary of some of the issues and the people who have stood up – across differences – to fight for equality.

It is a tool that will inform and inspire, that will create, for the reader, a sense of connection to the past, an understanding that they stand in the footsteps of others in a story of global solidarity.

And finally, this little book is also a call to action – a reminder that through small steps and larger ones, we can all make a difference and create a better world for all.

The pages that follow deliver a scrapbook timeline of the women's movement. It showcases the strident women who have pioneered key achievements, while infographic maps emphasize the campaign's international scope. Dividing this history into three waves and colour-coding facts according to continent, the timeline acknowledges that each period and place has its distinct identity while also emphasizing continuity.

Out of the first wave's push for legal equality bloomed the activism of the second, addressing expectations of gender and entrenched discrimination. As the third wave continued this fight, emphasizing inclusivity and intersectionality, feminism's purpose and drive has gathered increasing numbers to the cause.

Given that feminism is a movement whose history spans centuries and continents, this book can't hope to be comprehensive. But it does aspire to give a flavour of its central achievements, intimate a sense of its global breadth and, above all, reveal the solidarity that has always formed its heart.

Together, we have fought for women's rights. Together, we have worked for emancipation and equality. There are many women whose contributions to the movement could not be featured in this short book, but their bravery, determination and singularity should not go unsung. Feminism is a transnational movement; its champions are many and its successes are shared.

The Women's March in 2017 was attended by seven million protestors in more than 20 countries across the world. It made the resounding statement: in the the twenty-first century, feminism has only got bigger, better and stronger.

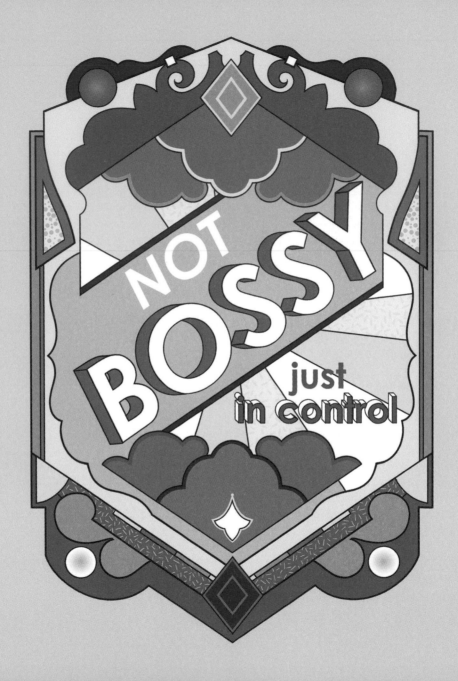

1 First-wave Feminism

1840s onwards

Demanding equal citizenship, women rally together to campaign for:
- suffrage
- property rights
- education
- birth control

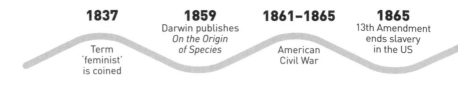

1837
Term
'feminist'
is coined

1859
Darwin publishes
*On the Origin
of Species*

1861–1865
American
Civil War

1865
13th Amendment
ends slavery
in the US

NOTHING ON EARTH WILL MAKE WOMEN GIVE WAY

The first wave marks the period when feminism resoundingly became a movement. Ahead of this there were forthright acts by individual women; there were groundbreaking political tracts; and there were strident 'protofeminists' who contested their political, economic and social rights. But the nineteenth century was the turning point: this is when 'feminist' activity – 'féminisme' having been coined by French philosopher Charles Fourier in 1837 – became collaborative and organized. Building associations, recruiting members across the globe and pioneering new forms of protest, first-wave campaigners transformed the international landscape of women's *de jure* rights – and they did it with collective clout.

The prevailing view at the time, the ideology of the 'separate spheres', held that a woman's role was in the home: her attitude was to be meek, nurturing and domestic. Women as well as men despaired to think of the societal repercussions of women being given a political voice: prophesying societal breakdown, they ridiculed those who dared to demand equality.

Campaigners recognized that nothing could be achieved without a say in parliament. From the 1890s onwards, the suffrage movement petitioned governments to grant women the franchise and the right to stand for election. While the campaign was not straightforward – notoriously plagued throughout by inner disagreements about

1900
Women compete
in Olympics for the
first time

1914
First
World War
begins

1920
Gandhi's non-cooperation
movement
in India

1920–1933
Prohibition
is enforced in
the US

1930s
Birth control now
legal in multiple
countries

tactics, such as when the British militant suffragettes split off from the moderate suffragists – it was successful, and universal suffrage is the most memorable legacy of the first wave. Emmeline Pankhurst's rousing pronouncement was substantiated: 'Nothing on earth and nothing in heaven will make women give way,' she called in a speech in 1914. And it didn't.

But the vote was not the only priority. Women had scant economic rights in the nineteenth century; the stifling legal doctrine of coverture treated any woman as effectively the property of her husband once she married. First-wave women's rights campaigners fought for the right to own and inherit their own money, to enter into contracts on their own terms and to become, for economic purposes, an individual.

Challenging the 'separate spheres' ideology meant ensuring equal access to education, if women were to enter into public life. We might take for granted women's right to receive an education, but it was only thanks to pioneering individuals who opened women's colleges and democratized the existing school and university systems that this became possible.

As the First World War loomed, one of the most controversial moves of the first wave was reformers' attempt to legalize the provision of contraception. Framing sexuality as an issue of public health, the birth control movement marked the beginning of an important transition period from the strict sexual mores of the Victoria era to a more liberal, permissive society, paving the way for the 'liberation' of the second wave.

FIRST WAVE IN CONTEXT

First-wave feminism emerged from a broader context of social justice movements. New ideologies were taking root and political and technological developments were redefining women's lives.

1840

THE ABOLITIONIST MOVEMENT

The movement to end slavery was closely twinned with the suffrage campaign in America and Europe, with the same women active in both campaigns. The women's rights movement even grew directly out of the mockery and discrimination these women faced in trying to speak out against slavery. The abolition movement achieved its successes sequentially. While Britain banned the trans-Atlantic slave trade in 1807, it was not until 1838 that all slaves in the British colonies were actually freed. Similarly, the US may have abolished the importation of slaves in 1807, but slavery itself was not definitely abolished until the Thirteenth Amendment in 1864.

1848

THE RISE OF COMMUNISM

The Communist Manifesto by Karl Marx and Friedrich Engels quickly became one of the world's most influential political documents. Proposing a radical vision of equality, the pamphlet galvanized movements for political and social change, culminating in the creation of the world's first socialist republic in 1917. Marx and Engels located the root of women's oppression within their role in the nuclear family, performing unpaid domestic labour. In the newly formed Soviet Union, the legal equality of the genders was made a priority; women entered the labour force in their thousands.

1914

THE LEGALIZATION OF CONTRACEPTION

Avowing to emancipate women 'from their slavery to the reproductive function', the birth control movement began in 1914 in response to restrictive legislation such as the Comstock Laws in the US, which had criminalized the distribution of information about contraceptives in the 1870s. Seeking to separate sexual activity from procreation, and educate women about reproductive health and sexual pleasure, pioneers including Aletta Jacobs in the Netherlands, Marie Stopes in Britain and Margaret Sanger in the US opened the first clinics, broke down taboos and brought reproductive rights into the political sphere.

1918

THE AFTERMATH OF THE FIRST WORLD WAR

Social trauma and political, cultural and economic transformation was the legacy of the First World War, which affected almost every continent – even those countries not directly involved in the conflict. In its aftermath, women were awarded the vote in several countries: during the conflict they had maintained the Home Front and entered new areas of the workforce, proving an ability to take on varied roles. These employment gains were not fully consolidated in the war's aftermath, however, hence the kindling of discontent that would spark the second wave.

1920s

THE FLAPPER AGE

A new definition of womanhood was born in the prosperity and cultural explosion of the Roaring Twenties: 'flappers' were women who posed a direct challenge to Victorian standards of respectability. They wore short skirts, drank alcohol, smoked cigarettes, bobbed their hair, listened to jazz, flirted outrageously and were otherwise reckless and independent. Their freedoms were reflected by their fashion: loose fitting dresses suitable for movement and dancing.

1929

ECONOMIC DEPRESSION AND RISE OF FASCISM

The Wall Street Crash spelled the beginning of the worst economic downturn in the history of the industrialized world, a period known as the Great Depression (1929–1939). If economic prosperity had heralded new freedoms for women, debt and poverty entailed its reverse. In Europe, the radical authoritarian form of governance known as fascism came to prominence. A fascist regime was installed in Italy in 1922 and the Nazi Party introduced a dictatorship in Germany in 1933, leading to an aggressive curtailing of women's rights: women were removed from the workforce, birth control was banned and abortion became a crime against the state.

EARLY FEMINIST PIONEERS

Before feminism became a mass movement, pioneering individuals around the world exposed inequalities, troubled the question of gender and challenged the status quo of patriarchy.

1405 Italian-French author **CHRISTINE DE PIZAN** wrote some of the first feminist literature, defending women in her books *The Book of the City of Ladies* and *The Treasure of the City of Ladies*. She was also the first woman in Europe successfully to make a living through her writing.

1700 **SOR JUANA INÉS DE LA CRUZ** was a Mexican scholar and Hieronymite nun. Her most famous work, the posthumously published *Respuesta a Sor Filotea de la Cruz* ('Reply to Sister Philotea'), is celebrated for its protofeminism, and advocates for women's access to education.

1761 **HEDVIG CHARLOTTA NORDENFLYCHT** was a Swedish poet and feminist. Unusually, she published under her own name, and used her poetry to defend the intelligence of women, most famously in *Fruentimrets försvar* ('To the Defense of Women').

1791 **OLYMPE DE GOUGES** was a French playwright and activist, whose writings were both feminist and abolitionist. She challenged male authority in her *Declaration of the Rights of Woman and the Female Citizen* (1791), in which she questioned the notion of male-female inequality. She was executed during the Reign of Terror for attacking the Revolutionary government's regime.

1792

MARY WOLLSTONECRAFT was a British women's rights advocate and author of *A Vindication of the Rights of Woman*, in which she argued that women must be educated to an equal level with men if they were to contribute equally.

1869

JOHN STUART MILL was a British philosopher and politician. In *The Subjection of Women* he attacked the notion that women are less capable than men, arguing for conditions of equality to be instated. As a Member of Parliament, Mill introduced an unsuccessful amendment to the Reform Bill to substitute the word 'person' in place of 'man'. He was the first MP to call for equal suffrage.

1845

MARGARET FULLER was a journalist, literary critic and women's rights advocate. She became America's first foreign war correspondent, while her book *Woman in the Nineteenth Century* is considered by many to be the first major American feminist work for its commitment to women's intellectual potential.

1881

ANNA MARIA MOZZONI was a feminist activist who published an Italian translation of John Stuart Mill's *The Subjection of Women*. In 1881 she founded the Lega promotrice degli interessi femminili ('League for the Promotion of the Interests of Women') and was a leading figure in the campaign for women's suffrage in Italy.

1848

SENECA FALLS CONVENTION,
NEW YORK, US

IN PROTEST AT WOMEN'S
EXCLUSION FROM THE WORLD
ANTI-SLAVERY CONVENTION IN
LONDON IN 1840, LUCRETIA MOTT
AND ELIZABETH CADY STANTON
ORGANIZE THEIR OWN ASSEMBLY
OF 200 WOMEN AND 40 MEN. THEY
PASS 12 RESOLUTIONS CALLING
FOR SPECIFIC EQUAL RIGHTS FOR
WOMEN, INCLUDING, BY A NARROW
MAJORITY, THE DUTY TO SECURE
THE FRANCHISE.

WE HOLD THESE TRUTHS TO BE SELF-EVIDENT: THAT ALL MEN AND WOMEN ARE CREATED EQUAL.

ELIZABETH CADY STANTON (1815–1902)

ABOLITIONIST AND LEADING FIGURE OF
THE EARLY WOMEN'S RIGHTS MOVEMENT
IN AMERICA.

'Men, their rights, and nothing more; women, their rights, and nothing less.'

Susan B. Anthony's name is synonymous with the campaign for women's suffrage in America. Born into a Quaker family, whose commitment to social equality extended to her own education, Susan embarked early on a career in social reform, collecting signatures for an anti-slavery petition at the age of seventeen. She met Elizabeth Cady Stanton in 1851 and forged a friendship that would define the lives and careers of both women. In 1848 they organized the first women's rights convention at Seneca Falls. Later, in 1869, they co-founded the National Woman Suffrage Association, which merged to become the National American Woman Suffrage Association in 1888. Susan led the group until 1900 and travelled extensively in support of the movement, giving as many as a hundred speeches a year. She died before the Nineteenth Amendment in 1920, but her legacy lives on. She became the first woman to be represented on a dollar coin in 1879.

Susan B. Anthony
AMERICAN

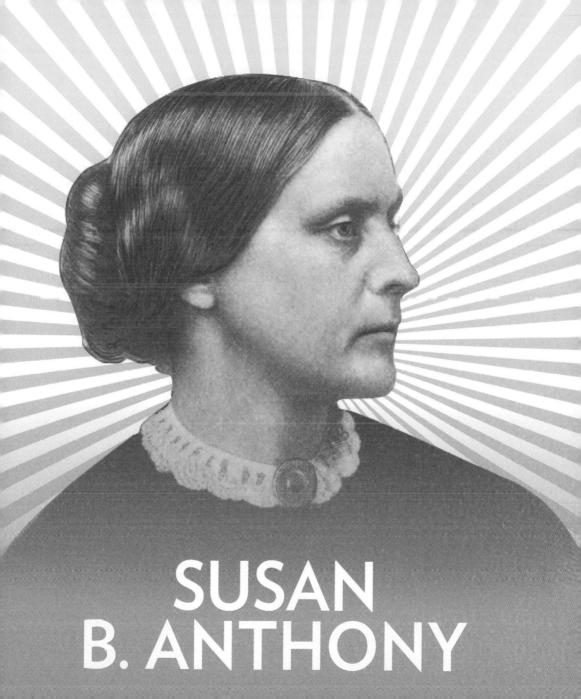

SUSAN
B. ANTHONY

1873

1878

SWEDEN

ANNA HIERTA-RETZIUS AND ELLEN ANCKARSVÄRD ESTABLISH THE MARRIED WOMEN'S PROPERTY RIGHTS ASSOCIATION, THE FIRST WOMEN'S RIGHTS ORGANIZATION IN SWEDEN, TO CAMPAIGN FOR AN END TO COVERTURE.

FRANCE

ORGANIZED BY MARIA DERAISMES, THE FIRST INTERNATIONAL CONGRESS OF WOMEN'S RIGHTS CONVENES IN PARIS. IT PASSES SEVEN RESOLUTIONS, INCLUDING THE DECLARATION 'ADULT WOMAN IS THE EQUIVALENT OF ADULT MAN'.

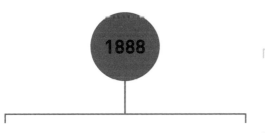

1888

1889

US

SUSAN ANTHONY AND ELIZABETH CADY STANTON HELP TO FOUND THE INTERNATIONAL COUNCIL OF WOMEN (ICW) TO CAMPAIGN FOR WOMEN'S RIGHTS INTERNATIONALLY. 53 ORGANIZATIONS FROM NINE COUNTRIES ATTEND THE FIRST MEETING.

NETHERLANDS

WILHEMINA DRUCKER FOUNDS THE FIRST WOMEN'S ORGANIZATION IN THE NETHERLANDS, THE FREE WOMEN'S ASSOCIATION. THIS BODY PLAYS A KEY ROLE IN EXPORTING FEMINISM TO BELGIUM: ACTIVELY ENDORSED BY DRUCKER, THE BELGIAN LEAGUE OF WOMEN'S RIGHTS IS ESTABLISHED IN 1892.

EARLY FEMINIST LITERATURE

Before feminist theory, women writers published influential texts across the genres of fiction and non-fiction which argued for women's independence and challenged patriarchal thinking.

1871 Under the male pseudonym **GEORGE ELIOT,** British author Mary Anne Evans publishes *Middlemarch*. Among the novel's achievements is the complex character Dorothea, a heroine whose struggles within the web of English society raise enduring questions about the status of women, the nature of marriage and the question of female sacrifice.

1873 One of the most respected Polish writers of her generation, **ELIZA ORZESZKOWA** publishes her novel *Marta,* which follows the misfortunes of a woman who is left destitute following the death of her husband. She tries repeatedly to secure employment to support herself and her daughter, but time and time again is turned away and told that men are preferable as employees.

1879 Norwegian playwright **HENRIK IBSEN** offers a daring critique of the institution of marriage and the suffocations of domesticity in his play *A Doll's House.* Portraying the struggles of housewife Nora to be treated as an individual and not as a petted doll, the play provoked debates worldwide about women's role in society and inspired feminists from Europe to Japan.

1892 American author **CHARLOTTE PERKINS GILMAN** publishes her provocative short story *The Yellow Wallpaper*, a coruscating attack on the gender roles of the period, especially with regard to women's mental health. With gothic intensity, the story follows the deterioration of protagonist Jane as she descends into madness, having been confined to her bedroom by her doctor husband for 'nerves' and forbidden to write.

1909

Canadian activist **NELLIE MCCLUNG** publishes her fourth book, *In Times Like These*, which develops a sophisticated series of arguments as to why women deserve the franchise, debunking popular myths and answering common objections.

1909

ALEXANDRA KOLLONTAI was the most prominent woman in the Soviet administration, the only woman elected to the Central Committee. While she played a central role in founding the Women's Department, through which she was able to introduce abortion and divorce on demand for the women of the Soviet Union, she was also an active journalist and theorist. She published *The Social Basis of the Woman Question* in 1909, a pamphlet which explores the origins of women's economic oppression.

1910

Swedish writer and suffragist **ELLEN KEY** publishes *Love and Marriage*, a treatise on motherhood in which she promotes birth control, argues for state subsidies for all mothers, including unmarried women, and maintains that 'love is moral even without legal marriage, but marriage is immoral without love.'

1929

British writer **VIRGINIA WOOLF** publishes her most enduring and powerful feminist essay, *A Room of One's Own*. Based on a series of lectures she gave to the literary societies of Newnham and Girton Colleges, Cambridge, the essay justifies the need for women to possess both a literal and figurative space within which to find financial and intellectual freedom. A landmark in feminist thought, the essay has never been out of print.

'Woman shall not be free [if] ... she doesn't show herself to be the self-assured, proud woman who wants to liberate herself from her shackles.'

Dutch politician and writer Wilhelmina Drucker was a driving force in the advancement of women's rights in the Netherlands. Born to unmarried parents, she took up her mother's profession as a seamstress but soon began attending meetings held by various socialist parties and organizations in Amsterdam. Influenced by socialism, and by her own experience with the struggles of unmarried women, she started writing under a pseudonym, exposing moral double standards and advocating for women's rights. Drucker founded the VVV (Free Women's Association) in 1889. In later years, she founded the weekly magazine *Evolutie* ('Evolution') and lectured on women's rights throughout the country, participating in the OV, the Women's Mutual Protection Society, which worked for the protection of unmarried mothers and their children.

Wilhelmina Drucker
DUTCH

1847–1925

WILHELMINA
DRUCKER

LEGALIZING PROPERTY RIGHTS

The women's rights movement helped to gain married women economic independence. Women also gained equal inheritance rights, although this fight is not yet over: several countries (for example, Tunisia) have yet to grant these rights.

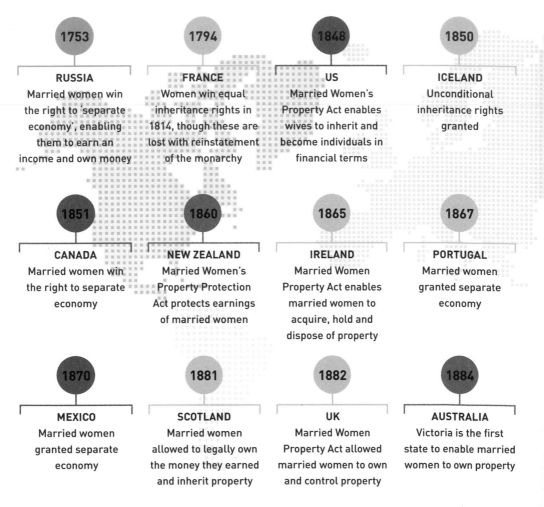

1753

RUSSIA

Married women win the right to 'separate economy', enabling them to earn an income and own money

1794

FRANCE

Women win equal inheritance rights in 1814, though these are lost with reinstatement of the monarchy

1848

US

Married Women's Property Act enables wives to inherit and become individuals in financial terms

1850

ICELAND

Unconditional inheritance rights granted

1851

CANADA

Married women win the right to separate economy

1860

NEW ZEALAND

Married Women's Property Protection Act protects earnings of married women

1865

IRELAND

Married Women Property Act enables married women to acquire, hold and dispose of property

1867

PORTUGAL

Married women granted separate economy

1870

MEXICO

Married women granted separate economy

1881

SCOTLAND

Married women allowed to legally own the money they earned and inherit property

1882

UK

Married Women Property Act allowed married women to own and control property

1884

AUSTRALIA

Victoria is the first state to enable married women to own property

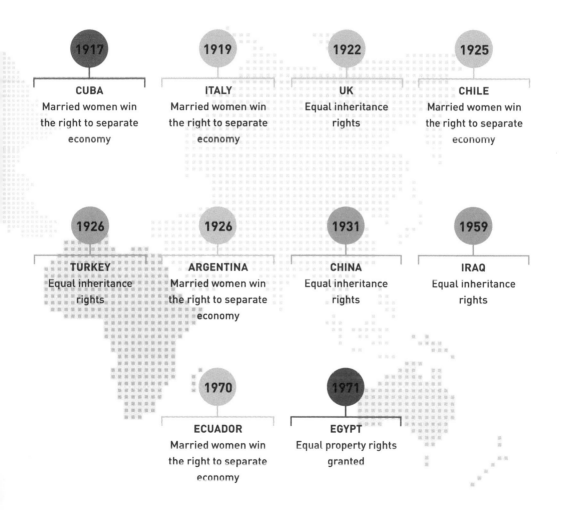

1917

CUBA
Married women win
the right to separate
economy

1919

ITALY
Married women win
the right to separate
economy

1922

UK
Equal inheritance
rights

1925

CHILE
Married women win
the right to separate
economy

1926

TURKEY
Equal inheritance
rights

1926

ARGENTINA
Married women win
the right to separate
economy

1931

CHINA
Equal inheritance
rights

1959

IRAQ
Equal inheritance
rights

1970

ECUADOR
Married women win
the right to separate
economy

1971

EGYPT
Equal property rights
granted

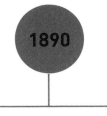

1890

US

THE NATIONAL WOMAN
SUFFRAGE ASSOCIATION
MERGES WITH ITS RIVAL
TO FORM THE NATIONAL
AMERICAN WOMAN
SUFFRAGE ASSOCIATION.
IT BECOMES THE LARGEST
VOLUNTARY ORGANIZATION
IN AMERICA, WITH
A MEMBERSHIP OF
TWO MILLION.

1903

UK

EMMELINE PANKHURST
FOUNDS THE WOMEN'S
SOCIAL AND POLITICAL
UNION (WSPU), A WOMEN-
ONLY ORGANIZATION THAT
FAVOURS DIRECT ACTION
AND CIVIL DISOBEDIENCE,
OR 'DEEDS NOT WORDS'.
THEY BECOME KNOWN AS
THE SUFFRAGETTES.

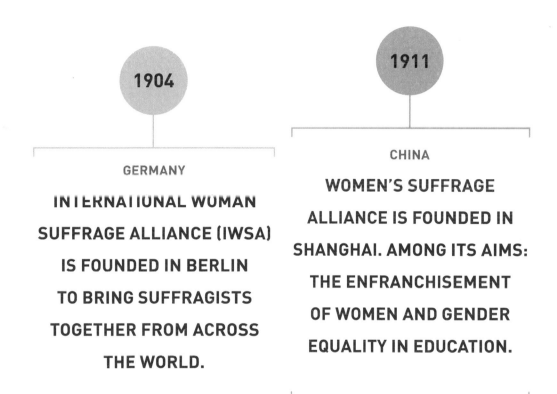

1904

GERMANY

INTERNATIONAL WOMAN SUFFRAGE ALLIANCE (IWSA) IS FOUNDED IN BERLIN TO BRING SUFFRAGISTS TOGETHER FROM ACROSS THE WORLD.

1911

CHINA

WOMEN'S SUFFRAGE ALLIANCE IS FOUNDED IN SHANGHAI. AMONG ITS AIMS: THE ENFRANCHISEMENT OF WOMEN AND GENDER EQUALITY IN EDUCATION.

'Courage calls to courage everywhere.'

The leader of the suffragists, Millicent Fawcett was one of Britain's foremost women's rights campaigners. She fought tirelessly for the franchise using the tactics of peaceful demonstration and political lobbying. Younger sister to Britain's first female doctor, Elizabeth Garrett Anderson, Fawcett entered the political fray at a young age, organizing signatures for the first petition for women's suffrage when she was nineteen. In 1907, she became president of the National Union of Women's Suffrage Societies, the largest organization of its kind with a membership of more than 50,000. She held the post for twelve years and lived to see women granted universal suffrage in 1928. Today her legacy lives on via the Fawcett Society, the UK's leading women's rights charity, which was renamed in her honour in 1953. She also became the first woman to be commemorated with a statue in London's Parliament Square in 2018.

Millicent Fawcett

BRITISH

1847–1929

MILLICENT
FAWCETT

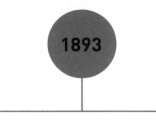

1893

**KATE SHEPPARD PRESENTS
A PETITION FOR WOMEN'S
SUFFRAGE TO PARLIAMENT
WITH 31,872 WOMEN'S
SIGNATURES. THE BILL
PASSED IN AUGUST, AND
NEW ZEALAND BECAME THE
FIRST COUNTRY TO LEGALIZE
UNIVERSAL SUFFRAGE.**

"

WE ARE TIRED OF HAVING A 'SPHERE' DOLED OUT TO US, AND BEING TOLD THAT ANYTHING OUTSIDE THAT SPHERE IS 'UNWOMANLY'... WE MUST BE OURSELVES AT ALL RISKS.

KATE SHEPPARD (1838–1934)
ADVOCATE FOR WOMEN'S SUFFRAGE AND
FIRST PRESIDENT OF NEW ZEALAND'S
NATIONAL COUNCIL OF WOMEN

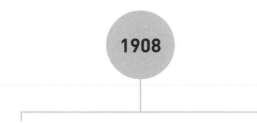

1908

FRANCE

INSPIRED BY THE BRITISH SUFFRAGETTES, HUBERTINE AUCLERT SYMBOLICALLY DESTROYS A BALLOT BOX IN THE MUNICIPAL ELECTIONS IN PARIS. SHE CONDEMNS 'UNISEXUAL SUFFRAGE'.

1910

UK

A WSPU MARCH SEES 300 SUFFRAGETTES, INCLUDING DR ELIZABETH GARRETT ANDERSON AND PRINCESS SOPHIA DULEEP SINGH, MARCH ON PARLIAMENT. THE WOMEN ARE CONFRONTED, ABUSED AND BADLY BEATEN BY POLICE IN WHAT BECOMES KNOWN AS THE BLACK FRIDAY DEMONSTRATION.

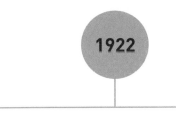

1922

UK

XIANG JINGYU LEADS A STRIKE OF 10,000 FEMALE WORKERS IN SHANGHAI'S SILK FACTORIES TO DEMAND BETTER PAY AND WORKING CONDITIONS IN THE FIRST MAJOR INDUSTRIAL ACTION BY WOMEN IN CHINA'S HISTORY.

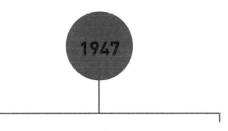

1947

NIGERIA

ACTIVIST FUNMILAYO RANSOME-KUTI LEADS 10,000 WOMEN TO MARCH ON THE PALACE OF THE ALAKE. THEY SING AND DANCE IN PROTEST AGAINST THE AUTHORITIES AND DEMAND AN END TO TAXATION WITHOUT DEMORACTIC REPRESENTATION.

'I have no rights, therefore, I have no taxes; I do not vote, I do not pay.'

The French trailblazer Hubertine Auclert was a fierce advocate of women's suffrage at a time when the mainstream of French feminism considered this stance too radical. She founded France's first suffrage league, *Le Suffrage des femmes*, in 1876 and experimented with a variety of tactics in her campaign to win the vote. Her most famous protest in the elections of May 1908 was destroying a ballot box, mimicking the tactics of the British suffragettes. She also ran as an illegal candidate for parliament, edited a militant newspaper, organized a tax boycott and several parades, and interrupted marriage ceremonies, warning the brides of the rights they were forfeiting. She is also credited with having been the first advocate of women's rights to call herself a 'feminist'.

Hubertine Auclert

FRENCH

1848–1914

SUFFRAGE FÉMIN...

HUBERTINE
AUCLERT

WHEN WOMEN WON THE RIGHT TO VOTE ACROSS THE WORLD

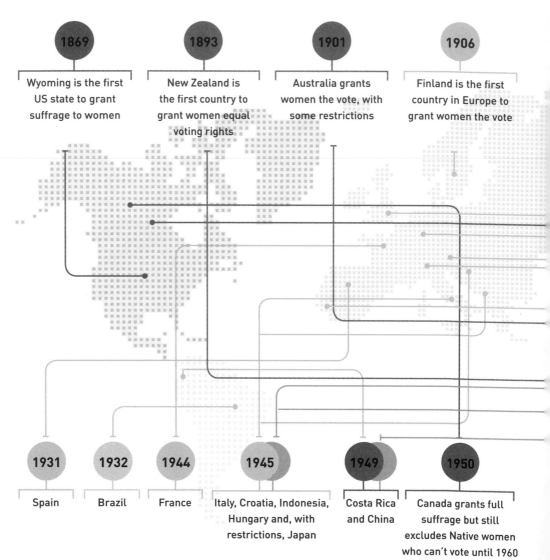

1869
Wyoming is the first US state to grant suffrage to women

1893
New Zealand is the first country to grant women equal voting rights

1901
Australia grants women the vote, with some restrictions

1906
Finland is the first country in Europe to grant women the vote

1931
Spain

1932
Brazil

1944
France

1945
Italy, Croatia, Indonesia, Hungary and, with restrictions, Japan

1949
Costa Rica and China

1950
Canada grants full suffrage but still excludes Native women who can't vote until 1960

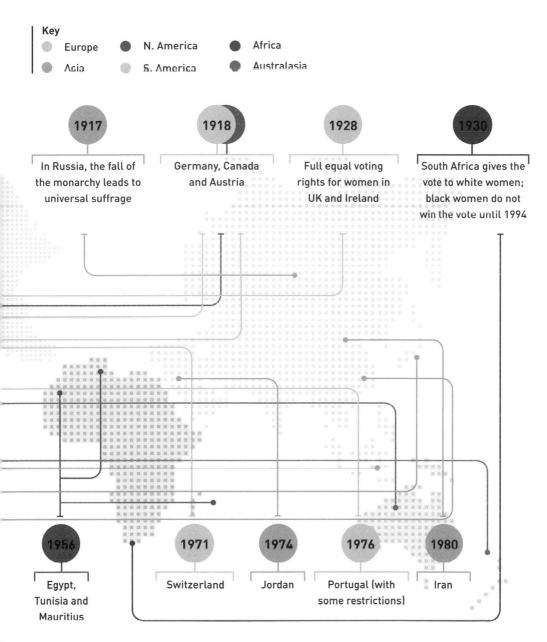

Key
- Europe
- N. America
- Africa
- Asia
- S. America
- Australasia

1917
In Russia, the fall of the monarchy leads to universal suffrage

1918
Germany, Canada and Austria

1928
Full equal voting rights for women in UK and Ireland

1930
South Africa gives the vote to white women; black women do not win the vote until 1994

1956
Egypt, Tunisia and Mauritius

1971
Switzerland

1974
Jordan

1976
Portugal (with some restrictions)

1980
Iran

1869

UK

IN PROTEST AT BEING PREVENTED FROM STUDYING MEDICINE, A GROUP OF WOMEN FORM 'THE EDINBURGH SEVEN'. RECEIVING THE ENDORSEMENT OF CHARLES DARWIN, THEY WIN NATIONAL SUPPORT AND THE UK MEDICAL ACT IS INTRODUCED IN 1876, ENABLING WOMEN TO QUALIFY AS DOCTORS.

1870

SPAIN

THE *ASOCIACIÓN PARA LA ENSEÑANZA DE LA MUJER* IS FOUNDED. PROMOTING EDUCATION FOR WOMEN, IT ESTABLISHES SECONDARY SCHOOLS AND TRAINING COLLEGES ALL OVER SPAIN, OPENING UP SECONDARY AND HIGHER EDUCATION TO WOMEN FOR THE FIRST TIME.

RUSSIA

ANNA FILOSOFOVA, NADEZHDA STASOVA, AND MARIIA TRUBNIKOVA, TOGETHER KNOWN AS THE 'TRIUMVIRATE', CREATE THE BESTUZHEV COURSES. THIS GAVE THE COUNTRY'S WOMEN RELIABLE ACCESS TO HIGHER EDUCATION FOR THE FIRST TIME.

CHINA

PEKING UNIVERSITY ACCEPTS ITS FIRST FEMALE STUDENTS, AND IS SOON FOLLOWED BY UNIVERSITIES ACROSS CHINA.

WOMEN IN EDUCATION

In many countries today, more women graduate from university than men, but that wasn't always the case. Below we showcase the women who triumphed despite discrimination and the dearth of opportunity, earning degrees, establishing women's colleges and gaining doctorates.

1608 Spaniard **JULIANA MORELL** is the first woman in the world to earn a law degree. She obtained her law doctorate in Avignon, having she presented her law thesis at the papal palace before a distinguished audience.

1732 Italian **LAURA BASSI** is the first woman to teach at a university, when she becomes a professor of physics at the University of Bologna.

1787 German **DOROTHEA SCHLÖZER** is the first German woman to earn a PhD at the Georg-August Universität Göttingen.

1861 In 1861 **JULIE-VICTOIRE DAUBIÉ** becomes the first woman to graduate from the University of Lyon, to which she was admitted on the strength of her essay 'The Poor Woman in the 19th Century. Female Conditions and Resources'. She became a journalist and continued to write about women's conditions, advocating for their rights until her death.

1788 **AURORA LILJENROTH** is the first woman to graduate in Sweden from Visingsö Gymnasium, graduating in 'all sciences' even though the gymnasium was not officially open to women.

1869 **EMILY DAVIES, BARBARA BODICHON** and **LADY STANLEY OF ALDERLEY** found Girton College, the first women's college at Cambridge University, which won't be officially affiliated with the university until 1948.

1870   **ADA KEPLEY** was the first woman to graduate with a law degree in America from what is today Northwestern University School of Law. She was initially prohibited from practising by state law that prevented women from working in the 'learned professions' but this was overturned in 1881.

1874   Russian mathematician **SOFIA KOVALEVSKAYA** is the first woman in Europe to earn a doctorate in mathematics from the University of Göttingen in Germany. She also becomes the first woman to be appointed to a full professorship in Northern Europe.

1904   **MILLICENT MACKENZIE** is appointed as Assistant Professor of Education at the University College of South Wales and Monmouthshire (part of the University of Wales), the first female professor in the UK..

1907   Iranian educator **TUBA AZMUDEH** establishes the first school for girls in Iran. At the time, girls were not usually educated outside of the home and it had been illegal for girls to attend school until 1896. Despite continual criticism and even death threats, Azmudeh expanded the school and the curriculum offering literary classes to adult women.

1924   Danish **NINA BANG** is appointed Minister for Education, becoming the first female minister in Europe. She worked to democratize the Danish school system, as well as to improve teacher training.

1931   **JANE BOLIN** graduates, becoming the first African-American woman to receive her degree from Yale Law School. She went on to become the first African-American woman to join the New York City Bar Association and the first African-American woman to serve as a judge in the US.

1882

1918

NETHERLANDS

UK

DUTCH PHYSICIAN ALETTA JACOBS OPENS THE WORLD'S FIRST BIRTH CONTROL CLINIC IN AMSTERDAM. FOR THE FIRST TIME A WOMAN COULD HAVE A CONTRACEPTIVE FITTED WITHOUT REQUIRING PERMISSION FROM HER HUSBAND.

MARIE STOPES PUBLISHES THE SEX MANUAL *MARRIED LOVE* WHICH BREAKS TABOOS FOR ITS PORTRAYAL OF WOMEN'S SEXUAL NEEDS. IT RAPIDLY SOLD OUT AND WAS IN ITS SIXTH PRINTING WITHIN A FORTNIGHT.

"

NO WOMAN CAN CALL HERSELF FREE WHO DOES NOT OWN AND CONTROL HER BODY. NO WOMAN CAN CALL HERSELF FREE UNTIL SHE CAN CHOOSE CONSCIOUSLY WHETHER SHE WILL OR WILL NOT BE A MOTHER.

MARGARET SANGER (1879–1976)

AMERICAN NURSE AND ACTIVIST WHO
POPULARIZED THE TERM 'BIRTH CONTROL'

'In the beginning, woman was truly the sun ... Now she is the moon, a wan and sickly moon, dependent on another, reflecting another's brilliance'.

Hiratsuka was a journalist, writer and political activist. In 1911 she founded the all-women literary magazine *Seitō* ('Bluestocking'), which incorporated essays and discussions about women's social position and broke taboos surrounding female sexuality and abortion. Hiratsuka's publications include essays such as 'To the Women of the World', which famously rejected that woman's role was to be exclusively a good wife and mother. Her statements were too outspoken for the Japanese state, which began censoring the magazine until it shut down in 1916. While it only lasted five years, *Seitō* was instrumental in inspiring the Japanese feminist movement. Continuing to fight for women's rights, Hiratsuka co-founded the New Women's Association in 1920, which overturned a regulation preventing women access to and participation in political activities. She kept writing and lecturing throughout her life.

Hiratsuka Raicho
JAPANESE

1886–1971

HIRATSUKA
RAICHO

2 Second-wave Feminism

1960s onwards

In the continuing fight
for equality, the personal
is political:

- employment rights
- reproductive rights
- challenging patriarchy

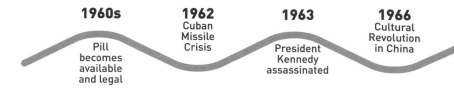

1960s
Pill becomes available and legal

1962
Cuban Missile Crisis

1963
President Kennedy assassinated

1966
Cultural Revolution in China

I AM NOT FREE WHILE ANY WOMAN IS UNFREE

Broadening the parameters of the fight for equality to the home, the workplace and reproductive rights, the second wave aimed at redefining gender roles and upturning patriarchal systems and values.

A woman in the 1960s could legally be paid less than a man in the same job. Across the globe, feminists fought to challenge this blatant inequality and redefine women's relationship with the workplace. In Iceland, women won the right to 'equal pay for equal work' in 1961; in the US, in 1963. These hard-won gains opened up new horizons of opportunity, reflected in growing numbers of women rising to the top of traditionally male-dominated fields. In 1970 in Sri Lanka, Sirimavo Bandaranaike made history, becoming the world's first woman to be elected head of state.

Where the first wave removed legal obstacles to gender equality, the second galvanized a social and cultural revolution alongside parallel civil rights movements: entrenched ideas about a woman's 'place' were disparaged and dismantled. In France, Simone de Beauvoir's *The Second Sex* (1945) was pivotal in teaching her readers radically to review the construct of womanhood, exposing its reliance on tropes of subservience, inferiority and deviance from the male 'norm'.

1966
Assassination of Martin Luther King

1969
Stonewall Riots in New York City

1979
China adopts one-child policy

1981
The AIDS epidemic officially begins

1989
Fall of the Berlin Wall and collapse of the Soviet bloc

In the US, Betty Friedan's *The Feminine Mystique* (1963) played a similarly important role, attacking the notion that marriage, housework and children were all a woman needed to find fulfilment, to the exclusion of education, a career or a political voice. Together these texts and others came to announce the new academic discipline of feminist theory, the first organized study of gender inequalities.

Women's Liberation movements carried these ideas over into direct action, mass protests, boycotts and strikes. In Iceland, women made an emphatic statement of determination when 90 per cent of women refused to work, cook, clean and look after children in 1975, driving home their importance to both economy and society. While employment legislation enabled women to seek alternatives roles outside of housewifery, gains in both divorce and reproductive rights meant a radical rethinking of the traditional structure of relationships. From Simone Veil to Alice Schwarzer, feminists fought for women's jurisdiction over their own bodies: the right to have an abortion and to receive cheap, easy access to contraception. The sexual revolution reframed female sexuality as defiant, bold and audacious.

By the 1970s, feminism had entered the mainstream. The United Nations organized the first of four world conferences to focus solely on women's rights in a move to empower women and girls across the globe. This carried over into action the sentiment that Audre Lorde had powerfully expressed: 'I am not free while any woman is unfree.'

SECOND WAVE IN CONTEXT

Redefined by another World War, second-wave feminism was shaped enormously by the release of the pill and changes in social mores, while mass unrest inspired its methods.

1945

THE AFTERMATH OF THE SECOND WORLD WAR
The deadliest conflict in human history, the Second World War rewrote the structure of the globe. In its aftermath, the United Nations was established to prevent future conflict. The war itself changed the role and expectations of women, many of whom had worked as labourers or nurses or served in combat. At the same time, the war's end heralded a new era of political tension: the rivalry and suspicion of the Cold War.

1960

THE SOCIAL IMPACT OF BIRTH CONTROL
Developed in the 1950s by American biologist Dr Gregory Pincus, the contraceptive pill ushered in a social and sexual revolution, offering women the freedom from unwanted pregnancy and control of their bodies, relationships and careers.

1962

THE SWINGING SIXTIES
Exuberant, optimistic, hedonistic, the sixties was the golden age of popular culture, driven by the postwar economic boom and the enthusiasm of a burgeoning youth culture. The Rolling Stones, The Beatles, The Who and The Kinks were some of the biggest names as a new popular music scene flourished, while changes in fashion and attitudes towards sexual freedom were complemented by the invention of the contraceptive pill. The miniskirt, marketed by Mary Quant in London from 1966, was the icon of the times – a coquettish departure from the conservative, utilitarian designs of the 1950s.

1964

CIVIL RIGHTS

In America and Canada, the Women's Liberation Movement grew directly out of the Civil Rights Movement: the campaign to secure equal constitutional and legal rights for African Americans, which reached its height in the mid-1960s. Galvanized by this parallel push for social justice, second-wave feminists took inspiration from their methods (sit-ins, marches and other non-violent protests) as well as from their success.

1968

SOCIAL AND POLITICAL UNREST

1968 was the year of explosive social upheaval and rebellion across the world. In Paris, Prague, Berlin, Chicago, Rome, London, Mexico City, Warsaw and beyond, social conflict erupted, predominantly characterized by popular rebellions against the military and bureaucratic elites. Historians disagree about the legacy of 1968, but many locate this year as the beginning of modern protest and the beginning of the end of the Cold War.

1969

SCIENCE & TECHNOLOGY

As one of several arenas in which Cold War rivalry played out, space exploration made huge advances in the sixties. Russian astronaut Yuri Gagarin became the first man in space in 1961, followed by the first woman in space, Valentina Tereshkova, in 1963. Fantasy fully became reality in 1969, when American Neil Armstrong became the first person to land on the moon in the Apollo 11 mission.

1979

WOMEN GAINING POWER

A measure of feminist success was given by the number of women elected leaders of state or government from the 1960s onwards. Sirimavo Bandaranaike was the first: she was elected Prime Minister of Sri Lanka in 1960, followed by Indira Gandhi, Prime Minister of India from 1966. Europe's first woman prime minister Margaret Thatcher was elected in 1979.

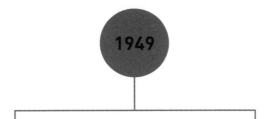

FRENCH PHILOSOPHER SIMONE DE BEAUVOIR PUBLISHES *THE SECOND SEX*, CONTENDING THAT WOMAN'S OPPRESSION STEMS FROM HER DESIGNATION AS 'OTHER': MAN IS DEFAULT AND OCCUPIES THE ROLE OF SELF OR SUBJECT, WHILE WOMAN IS THE OBJECT.

"

ONE IS NOT BORN, BUT RATHER BECOMES, A WOMAN.

SIMONE DE BEAUVOIR (1908–1986)
FRENCH WRITER AND PHILOSOPHER WHOSE
WRITINGS INSPIRED THE SECOND WAVE

"

SECOND-WAVE FEMINIST THEORY

Feminist theory is a discipline that seeks to understand the nature and structure of gender inequality. Highlighting the hold that patriarchal sexism continues to exert on our attitudes, it plays an important role in focusing efforts to end discrimination.

1963

BETTY FRIEDAN publishes *The Feminine Mystique*, a powerful study of the dissatisfaction experienced by 1950s housewives that condemns the prevailing conflation of femininity with passivity, and the assumption that women find fulfilment only through housework, marriage and child-rearing.

1970

Australian **GERMAINE GREER** forcefully enters the arena with the publication of *The Female Eunuch*, arguing that the social norms of marriage and family repress female sexuality, devitalizing women to the point of making them eunuchs. Combining polemic with research, the book becomes a key text of the second-wave feminist movement.

1970

American author **KATE MILLETT** releases *Sexual Politics*, a searing analysis of patriarchal power that becomes an important theoretical touchstone of the Women's Liberation Movement. Contending that men's institutionalized power over women is socially constructed as opposed to innate, she analyses the ways in which women are socialized into accepting patriarchal values and norms, and reveals women's complicity in male domination.

1973

Belgian-French psycholinguist **LUCE IRIGARAY** redefines psychoanalysis with her landmark work *Speculum of the Other Woman*. She considers various constructions of women in Western philosophy, and finds Western discourse has reduced woman to a male construct with no status of her own.

1974

Bulgarian-French philosopher **JULIA KRISTEVA** publishes *Revolution in Poetic Language*. She argues signification is composed of two elements, the symbolic (masculine; associated with structure) and the semiotic (feminine, rhythmic; associated with the mother and lacking differentiation). As a child moves into the realm of language, he or she moves away from the semiotic towards the symbolic, and feels the need to reject the mother figure.

1975

The American feminist film critic **LAURA MULVEY** coins the term 'male gaze' in her seminal essay 'Visual Pleasure and Narrative Cinema'. She argues that a controlling force in cinema is the depiction of the world from a heterosexual masculine perspective, which seeks gratification in the sexual objectification of women.

1978

British psychotherapist and social critic **SUSIE ORBACH** analyzes the psychology of dieting and compulsive eating in her pioneering anti-diet book *Fat is a Feminist Issue*. Considering the subconscious meanings of fatness and thinness, she explores our obsession with body image and makes the forceful argument that it is gender inequality that makes women fat.

1979

African-American writer and civil rights activist **AUDRE LORDE** delivers her paper 'The Master's Tools Will Never Dismantle the Master's House'. Her argument is that popular feminism will be just as oppressive as the patriarchy it is trying to overcome unless it acknowledges the voices and experiences of women of colour, lesbians and the working class.

1984

The radical African-American feminist **BELL HOOKS** publishes *Feminist Theory: From Margin to Center*. She argues that the goal of the feminist movement should not be to achieve equality in the current corrupt system of 'white-supremacist capitalist patriarchy'. Instead, feminists should organize to overturn the cultural framework of power and instantiate a version wherein oppression of others – whether on account of race, class or sex – is not necessary.

'Who knows what women can be when they are finally free to become themselves?'

Betty Friedan is widely regarded as the mother of second-wave feminism for her landmark document of the constraints imposed by traditional gender roles, *The Feminine Mystique* (1963). A psychology graduate, Friedan wrote the book having lived as a housewife and mother in the suburbs of New York for five years and undertaken extensive research. The book was an immediate success, selling three million copies on publication, and is credited with having drawn huge numbers to the feminist cause. Friedan went on to co-found and become the first president of the National Organization for Women (NOW), the largest women's movement organization in the US. In this role, Friedan campaigned for more women to be represented in government, for childcare centres for working mothers and for the legalization of abortion. In 1970 she organized the nationwide Women's Strike for Equality to commemorate fifty years since American women won the vote.

Betty Friedan
AMERICAN

1921–2016

BETTY FRIEDAN

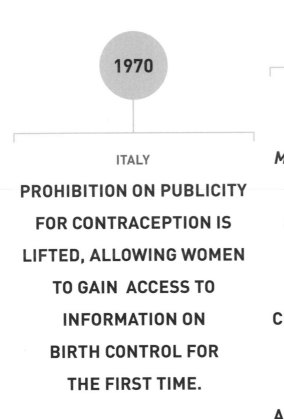

1970

ITALY

PROHIBITION ON PUBLICITY FOR CONTRACEPTION IS LIFTED, ALLOWING WOMEN TO GAIN ACCESS TO INFORMATION ON BIRTH CONTROL FOR THE FIRST TIME.

1971

FRANCE

343 WOMEN SIGN *LE MANIFESTE DES 343 SALOPES* ('THE MANIFESTO OF THE 343 WHORES') DECLARING THEY HAVE HAD AN ABORTION. THIS ACT OF CIVIL DISOBEDIENCE CALLED FOR THE LEGALIZATION OF ABORTION AND FREE ACCESS TO CONTRACEPTION. WRITTEN BY SIMONE DE BEAUVOIR, IT INSPIRED A SIMILAR DOCUMENT IN GERMANY.

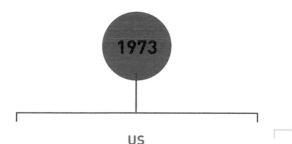

1973

US

THE US SUPREME COURT AFFIRMS THE LEGALITY OF A WOMAN'S RIGHT TO HAVE AN ABORTION IN THE HISTORIC ROE VS WADE CASE.

1975

FRANCE

SIMONE VEIL SUCCEEDS IN PASSING THE VOLUNTARY INTERRUPTION OF PREGNANCY ACT (THE VEIL LAW) WHICH LEGALIZES ABORTION FOR THE FIRST 12 WEEKS OF GESTATION.

'My claim as a woman is that my difference is taken into account; that I do not have to adapt to the male model.'

Politician Simone Veil led the battle to legalize abortion in France. Of Jewish descent, she survived the Holocaust despite being arrested and deported by German authorities in 1944, and then studied law and political sciences in Paris after the Liberation. After years practising as a lawyer and a magistrate she gained access to the Ministry of Justice, where she was able to improve the condition of women's prisons. Later, Veil served in the French national government as Minister of Health, and was the first female President of the European Parliament. She is chiefly remembered for the law that bears her name, the Loi Veil, which legalized abortion in 1975, but she is also responsible for the advancement of civil rights for women in terms of parental rights, adoption rights and the improvement of maternity benefit, childcare and health cover.

Simone Veil
FRENCH

1927-2017

SIMONE
VEIL

LEGALIZING ABORTION

The termination of a pregnancy has historically been illegal or restricted in most countries around the world. Second-wave feminists and beyond fought to see this changed.

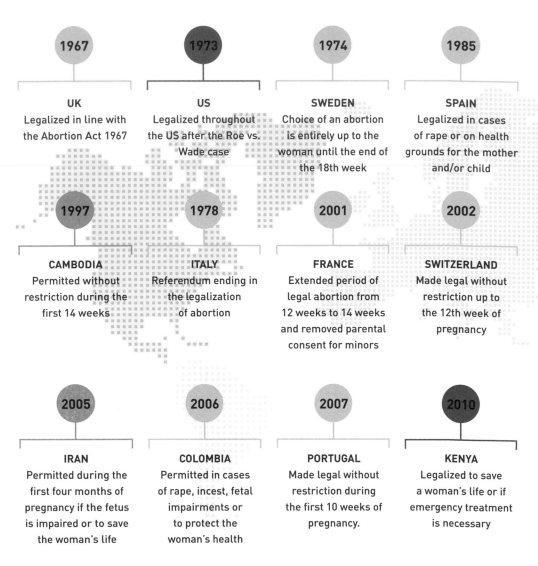

1967

UK
Legalized in line with the Abortion Act 1967

1973

US
Legalized throughout the US after the Roe vs. Wade case

1974

SWEDEN
Choice of an abortion is entirely up to the woman until the end of the 18th week

1985

SPAIN
Legalized in cases of rape or on health grounds for the mother and/or child

1997

CAMBODIA
Permitted without restriction during the first 14 weeks

1978

ITALY
Referendum ending in the legalization of abortion

2001

FRANCE
Extended period of legal abortion from 12 weeks to 14 weeks and removed parental consent for minors

2002

SWITZERLAND
Made legal without restriction up to the 12th week of pregnancy

2005

IRAN
Permitted during the first four months of pregnancy if the fetus is impaired or to save the woman's life

2006

COLOMBIA
Permitted in cases of rape, incest, fetal impairments or to protect the woman's health

2007

PORTUGAL
Made legal without restriction during the first 10 weeks of pregnancy.

2010

KENYA
Legalized to save a woman's life or if emergency treatment is necessary

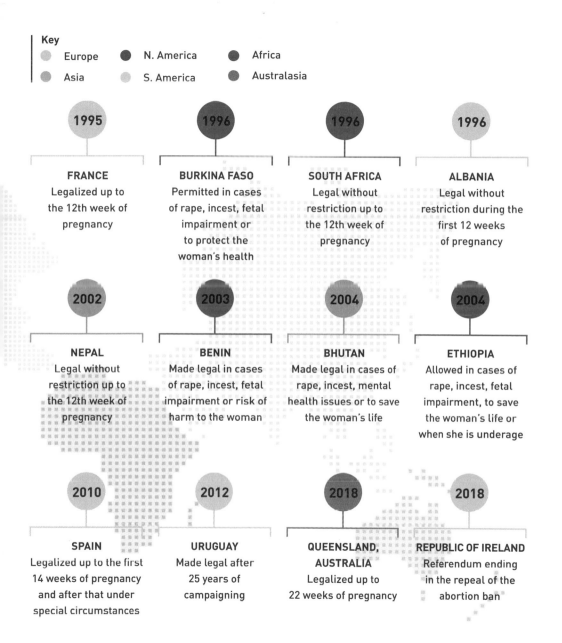

Key
- Europe
- Asia
- N. America
- S. America
- Africa
- Australasia

1995

FRANCE
Legalized up to the 12th week of pregnancy

1996

BURKINA FASO
Permitted in cases of rape, incest, fetal impairment or to protect the woman's health

1996

SOUTH AFRICA
Legal without restriction up to the 12th week of pregnancy

1996

ALBANIA
Legal without restriction during the first 12 weeks of pregnancy

2002

NEPAL
Legal without restriction up to the 12th week of pregnancy

2003

BENIN
Made legal in cases of rape, incest, fetal impairment or risk of harm to the woman

2004

BHUTAN
Made legal in cases of rape, incest, mental health issues or to save the woman's life

2004

ETHIOPIA
Allowed in cases of rape, incest, fetal impairment, to save the woman's life or when she is underage

2010

SPAIN
Legalized up to the first 14 weeks of pregnancy and after that under special circumstances

2012

URUGUAY
Made legal after 25 years of campaigning

2018

QUEENSLAND, AUSTRALIA
Legalized up to 22 weeks of pregnancy

2018

REPUBLIC OF IRELAND
Referendum ending in the repeal of the abortion ban

'Women may have learnt to admire the strength of men, yet they remain suspicious about the strength of other women.'

Possibly the most famous and controversial feminist in Germany, Alice Schwarzer was first introduced to the fight for women's rights while working as a journalist in France, a hotbed of civil rights battling. Here she met Simone de Beauvoir, Catherine Deneuve and Jeanne Moreau, all of whom were campaigning for abortion rights. Inspired by their methods, Schwarzer published an article in the magazine *Stern* in 1971, featuring 374 women who publicized their illegal abortions. The cause of great scandal, this article initiated a new wave of protests, yet only marked the beginning of her outspoken career. In 1977 Schwarzer founded her own magazine, *Emma*, and later started a feminist archive. She is an author of taboo-breaking books about women's sex lives, including *The Little Difference and its Great Consequences*.

Alice Schwarzer

GERMAN

1942–

ALICE
SCHWARZER

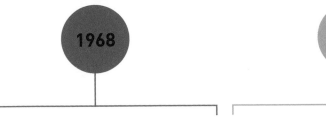

1968

1971

US

JAPAN

TO MAKE A STATEMENT ABOUT NORMATIVE BEAUTY STANDARDS AND THE OBJECTIFICATION OF WOMEN, 200 WOMEN'S LIBERATION PROTESTERS BOYCOTT THE MISS AMERICA CONTEST IN ATLANTIC CITY. CROWNING A SHEEP 'MISS AMERICA', THEY COMPARE THE PAGEANT TO LIVESTOCK COMPETITIONS.

LED BY MITSU TANAKA, THE GROUP TATAKAU ONNATACHI ORGANIZES A RALLY TO CAMPAIGN FOR ABORTION RIGHTS, WHICH LEADS TO THE ESTABLISHMENT OF THE CENTRE FOR WOMEN'S LIBERATION IN 1972. THIS SPACE IN TOKYO PROVIDES A FORUM FOR FEMINISTS TO EXCHANGE VIEWS AND A REFUGE FOR WOMEN IN NEED OF HELP.

1977

THE FIRST 'RECLAIM THE NIGHT' MARCH IS ORGANIZED IN LEEDS IN PROTEST AT THE YORKSHIRE RIPPER MURDERS AND THE POLICE STATEMENT THAT WOMEN SHOULD STAY OUT OF PUBLIC SPACES AFTER DARK. SOON AN INTERNATIONAL MOVEMENT TAKES OFF WITH NIGHT MARCHES AGAINST SEXUAL VIOLENCE IN ITALY, INDIA, GERMANY AND AUSTRALIA.

1979

US

ORGANIZED BY THE RADICAL FEMINIST GROUP 'WOMEN AGAINST PORNOGRAPHY' (WAP), 6,000 DEMONSTRATORS GATHERED IN TIMES SQUARE TO MARCH FOR THE CRIMINALIZING OF PORN. THE WAP GREW OUT OF EARLIER FEMINIST ANTI-VIOLENCE MEDIA CAMPAIGNS AND FOCUSED ON RAISING AWARENESS OF THE HARMS CAUSED BY PORN AND THE SEX INDUSTRY.

'A woman without a man is like a fish without a bicycle.'

Journalist, writer and feminist political activist Gloria Steinem is one of the most popular spokespersons for gender equality. Her career began writing freelance in New York, where she helped found the *New York Magazine* in 1968 and started to take an interest in politics and report on women's liberation movement campaigns. Steinem got involved in and spoke out for the legalization of abortion and her 1969 article 'After Black Power, Women's Liberation' put her firmly in the centre of feminist activism and became an essential reference point for the women's movement. Realizing the absence of a magazine that covered the women's cause, she co-founded *Ms.* in 1972, the world's first mass circulation feminist magazine. Steinem also helped to found the National Women's Political Caucus, a group that advocated for gender equality and for the increase of pro-equality women in elected office in America.

Gloria Steinem
AMERICAN

1952–

GLORIA
STEINEM

WOMEN IN PRINT

Committed to creating a canon of women's writing, the Women's Liberation Movement launched its own publishing houses, bookshops and magazines in the 1960s and '70s. Feminist journalism also flourished. We showcase a few examples below.

1970
The newly-formed **Boston Women's Health Book Collective** self-publishes the 193-page booklet *Women and Their Bodies*, which daringly encourages women to take charge of their own health and sexuality. It cost 75 cents. A year later, the title is changed to *Our Bodies, Ourselves* and the booklet quickly becomes the women's health bible. It has remained available ever since and has been published in more than 20 countries.

1970
The American publisher **Feminist Press** is established, reprinting feminist classics by writers such as Zora Neale Hurston and Charlotte Perkins Gilman and providing texts for the developing field of women's studies, including books by Barbara Ehrenreich and Grace Paley.

1972
A group of left-wing Belgian feminists publish *Le Petit livre rouge des Femmes* ('The Little Red Book of Women'), an analysis of patriarchal society with plans for an egalitarian, feminist alternative. The little book causes quite a noise on its initial release, selling 15,000 copies in its first few months. It is now available online and its ideas remain topical.

1972
A British collective founded by Rosie Boycott and Marsha Rowe publishes the iconic feminist magazine *Spare Rib*. Newsagents initially refuse to stock the publication but it soon becomes one of the most important publications in Britain in the 70s and 80s, celebrated for its forthright challenge to patriarchy and gender norms.

1972

American feminist Gloria Steinem founds *Ms. magazine*, the first mass circulation feminist publication, with a readership of over 400,000. It offers in-depth feminist analysis of national and international issues, as well as coverage of feminist events. Originally published monthly, the magazine is now a quarterly published by the Feminist Majority Foundation.

1973

Following a demonstration by Swedish Women's Liberation protestors, the publishing house Aschehoug is forced to publish a translation of the text *Frihet, jämlikhet och systerskap* ('Freedom, Equality and Sisterhood: A Handbook for Women') which provided a detailed action programme for addressing gender inequality.

1973

Leader of the French Liberation Movement, Antoinette Fouque launches her own publishing press, **Les Editions des Femmes.** Its programme remains influential and politically charged today, aimed at furthering women's rights in France and beyond. The press has actively contributed to the liberation of women who are oppressed or imprisoned.

1973

Meaning 'heroic war-like woman', Virago gives its name to **Virago Press**, founded in the UK by Australian writer and critic Carmen Callil. The imprint's mission is to champion women's voices across different genres, both new works and out-of-print texts, and remains one of the most important British feminists presses.

1976

Les Editions du Remue-Ménage is founded in Quebec. The name is a pun and means 'to make a lot of noise and move things around', generally invoking the idea of change, but '*ménage*' also means tidying up – an activity historically reserved for women. Their current logo is a broom, used by cleaners (and witches) to clean out prejudice, in a signifier of the fight for equality.

1977

German Alice Schwarzer sets up *EMMA*, Germany's seminal feminist magazine, to instigate debates on women's issues. The name plays on 'EM(M)ANCIPATION' and tackles themes such as family, politics, education, religion, the media and pornography.

1970

US

50,000 WOMEN MARCH THROUGH NEW YORK CITY AND COORDINATE DEMONSTRATIONS THROUGHOUT THE US IN A 'STRIKE FOR EQUALITY' AIMED AT A NATIONAL WORK STOPPAGE. WOMEN CEASED COOKING AND CLEANING TO DRAW ATTENTION TO THE UNEQUAL DISTRIBUTION OF DOMESTIC LABOUR.

1972

ITALY

CAMPAIGN IS LAUNCHED IN PADUA TO ACHIEVE RECOGNITION FOR THE UNPAID LABOUR OF HOUSEWORK AND CHILDCARE. THE MOVEMENT 'WAGES FOR HOUSEWORK' ORGANIZES PUBLIC DEBATES ON THE GENDERED ASPECTS OF LABOUR AND LEISURE.

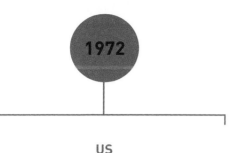

1972

US

AMERICAN SOCIALIST SELMA JAMES AND ITALIAN FEMINIST MARIAROSA DALLA COSTA PROPOSE THE INTERNATIONAL WAGES FOR HOUSEWORK CAMPAIGN. RESISTING THE IDEA OF GENDERED LABOUR, THE CAMPAIGN WORKED FOR THE RIGHT TO WORK OUTSIDE OF THE HOME, PARENTAL LEAVE AND PAYMENT FROM THE STATE FOR DOMESTIC WORK.

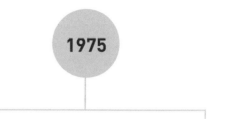

1975

ICELAND

90 PER CENT OF ALL WOMEN GO ON STRIKE TO DEMONSTRATE THEIR INDISPENSABLE CONTRIBUTION TO THE ECONOMY. THEY DEMAND EQUAL PAY AND BETTER EMPLOYMENT PRACTICE.

| LEGALIZING DIVORCE

As a result of women's campaigns for the transition of marriage from a religious sacrament to a civil union, divorce is now legal in every country of the world except two: the Philippines and Vatican City (the Philippines is likely to change this shortly). Here are the global dates when divorce became legal.

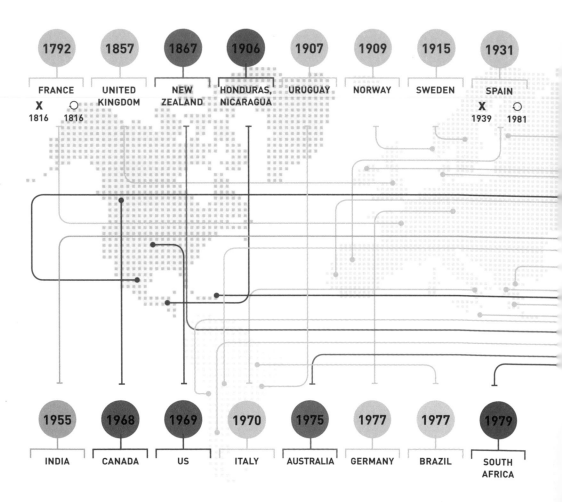

1792	1857	1867	1906	1907	1909	1915	1931
FRANCE	UNITED KINGDOM	NEW ZEALAND	HONDURAS, NICARAGUA	URUGUAY	NORWAY	SWEDEN	SPAIN

FRANCE
X   O
1816 1816

SPAIN
X   O
1939 1981

1955	1968	1969	1970	1975	1977	1977	1979
INDIA	CANADA	US	ITALY	AUSTRALIA	GERMANY	BRAZIL	SOUTH AFRICA

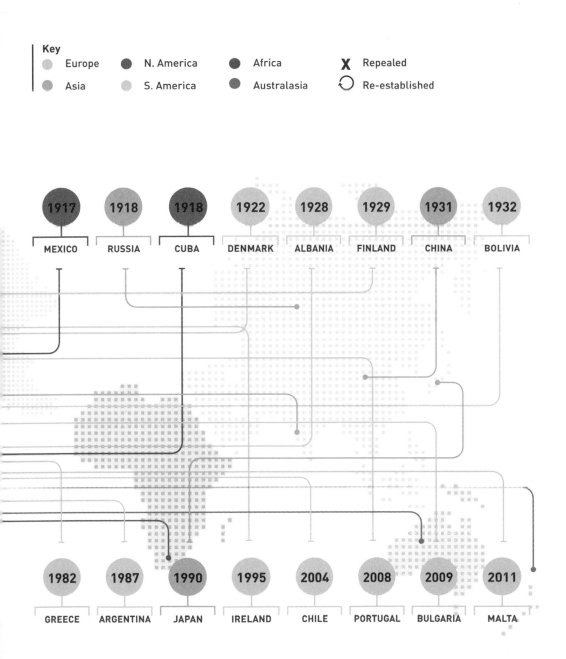

Key

- Europe
- Asia
- N. America
- S. America
- Africa
- Australasia
- **X** Repealed
- Re-established

1917 — MEXICO
1918 — RUSSIA
1918 — CUBA
1922 — DENMARK
1928 — ALBANIA
1929 — FINLAND
1931 — CHINA
1932 — BOLIVIA

1982 — GREECE
1987 — ARGENTINA
1990 — JAPAN
1995 — IRELAND
2004 — CHILE
2008 — PORTUGAL
2009 — BULGARIA
2011 — MALTA

1975

MEXICO

FIRST UNITED NATIONS WORLD CONFERENCE ON WOMEN MARKS THE FIRST CONFERENCE TO FOCUS SOLELY ON WOMEN'S ISSUES. THE UN NAMES 1975 INTERNATIONAL WOMEN'S YEAR AND ESTABLISHES THE UN DEVELOPMENT FUND FOR WOMEN.

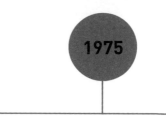

1975

US

TIME MAGAZINE AWARDS ITS PERSON OF THE YEAR TO 'AMERICAN WOMEN' ARGUING 1975 'WAS NOT SO MUCH THE YEAR OF THE WOMAN AS THE YEAR OF THE *WOMEN*'. THE MAGAZINE CELEBRATES 'THE EVERYDAY, USUALLY ANONYMOUS WOMAN WHO MOVED INTO THE MAINSTREAM OF JOBS, IDEAS AND POLICYMAKING'.

RIGHTS ARE NOT 'FOREVER': THEY MUST BE CHERISHED AND DEFENDED.

EMMA BONINO (1948–)
ITALIAN POLITICIAN WHO LED SUCCESSFUL
CAMPAIGNS TO LEGALIZE ABORTION
AND DIVORCE

THE FIRST DEMOCRATICALLY ELECTED FEMALE LEADERS

Women have set political precedents in more than 60 countries around the world, rising to the top of the political system.

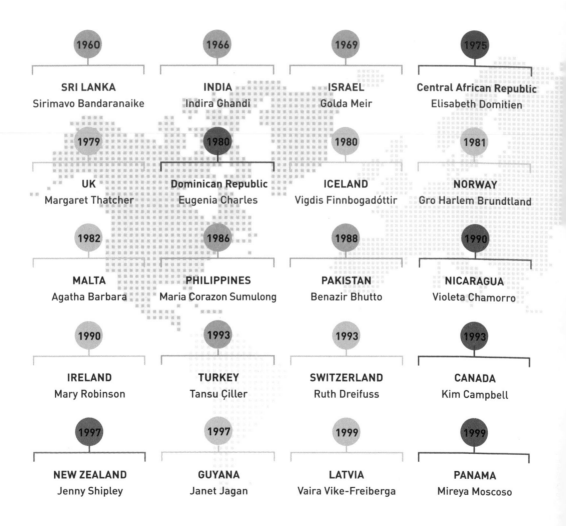

1960	1966	1969	1975
SRI LANKA Sirimavo Bandaranaike	**INDIA** Indira Ghandi	**ISRAEL** Golda Meir	**Central African Republic** Elisabeth Domitien

1979	1980	1980	1981
UK Margaret Thatcher	**Dominican Republic** Eugenia Charles	**ICELAND** Vigdis Finnbogadóttir	**NORWAY** Gro Harlem Brundtland

1982	1986	1988	1990
MALTA Agatha Barbara	**PHILIPPINES** Maria Corazon Sumulong	**PAKISTAN** Benazir Bhutto	**NICARAGUA** Violeta Chamorro

1990	1993	1993	1993
IRELAND Mary Robinson	**TURKEY** Tansu Çiller	**SWITZERLAND** Ruth Dreifuss	**CANADA** Kim Campbell

1997	1997	1999	1999
NEW ZEALAND Jenny Shipley	**GUYANA** Janet Jagan	**LATVIA** Vaira Vike-Freiberga	**PANAMA** Mireya Moscoso

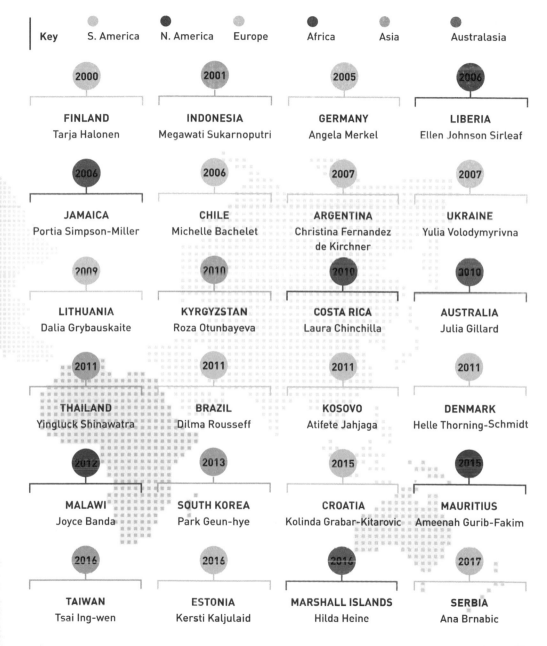

Key S. America N. America Europe Africa Asia Australasia

2000
FINLAND
Tarja Halonen

2001
INDONESIA
Megawati Sukarnoputri

2005
GERMANY
Angela Merkel

2006
LIBERIA
Ellen Johnson Sirleaf

2006
JAMAICA
Portia Simpson-Miller

2006
CHILE
Michelle Bachelet

2007
ARGENTINA
Christina Fernandez
de Kirchner

2007
UKRAINE
Yulia Volodymyrivna

2009
LITHUANIA
Dalia Grybauskaite

2010
KYRGYZSTAN
Roza Otunbayeva

2010
COSTA RICA
Laura Chinchilla

2010
AUSTRALIA
Julia Gillard

2011
THAILAND
Yingluck Shinawatra

2011
BRAZIL
Dilma Rousseff

2011
KOSOVO
Atifete Jahjaga

2011
DENMARK
Helle Thorning-Schmidt

2012
MALAWI
Joyce Banda

2013
SOUTH KOREA
Park Geun-hye

2015
CROATIA
Kolinda Grabar-Kitarovic

2015
MAURITIUS
Ameenah Gurib-Fakim

2016
TAIWAN
Tsai Ing-wen

2016
ESTONIA
Kersti Kaljulaid

2016
MARSHALL ISLANDS
Hilda Heine

2017
SERBIA
Ana Brnabic

WOMEN IN SCIENCE

Despite the tendency to see science as a male discipline, women have shaped our understanding of the cosmos since the earliest times, from Hypatia of Alexandria, the first recorded woman mathematician, who led the field in Ancient Egypt.

1903 — Polish-French physicist **MARIE CURIE** becomes the first woman to win a Nobel Prize. She first wins this in physics for her groundbreaking work on radioactivity. In 1911 she wins her second Nobel Prize in Chemistry, becoming the first person to win it twice.

1941 — Famous Hollywood filmstar **HEDY LAMARR** receives a patent for an early form of 'spread spectrum' telecommunications. Her invention, which she calls 'frequency hopping', was originally developed to prevent classified messages being intercepted during wartime. Its full significance will be realized in later decades: Lamarr's military technology paved the way for wifi, GPS and bluetooth.

1951 — British chemist **ROSALIND FRANKLIN** works on her X-ray diffraction images of DNA, which was intrinsic to Crick and Watson's discovery of DNA structure.

1963 — Russian Cosmonaut **VALENTINA TERESHKOVA** is the first woman to enter space in a mission that lasted almost three days. Tereshkova orbits Earth 48 times and still is the only woman to have been on a solo space mission. After the mission she serves as a member in the government both before and after the collapse of the Soviet Union.

1964

British Chemist **DOROTHY HODGKIN** is the first and only British woman to win the Nobel Prize for Chemistry for her development of protein crystallography. Former teacher to Margaret Thatcher, Hodgkin was able to determine the atomic structure of cholesterol, penicillin and vitamin B12. Her work significantly improved the treatment of diabetes.

1981

Ophthalmologist **PATRICIA BATH** becomes the first African-American woman doctor to receive a patent for a medical purpose. Bath is also co-founder of the American Institute for the Prevention of Blindness.

1991

American computer scientist and navy rear admiral **GRACE HOPPER** is awarded the National Medal of Technology. One of the first women to achieve a PhD in mathematics (1934), Grace was a pioneer of computer programming and worked on the development of the first functional computer, Mark I.

2015

Chinese chemist **PROFESSOR TU YOUYOU** wins the Nobel Prize in Physiology or Medicine for her discovery of the drugs artemisinin and dihydroartemisinin for the treatment of malaria. Her drugs have been used to treat 200 million patients, saving millions of lives.

2015

Moroccan Professor of Nuclear Physics **RAJAA CHERKAOUI EL MOURSLI** wins the L'Oréal-UNESCO For Women in Science Awards for her essential role in the discovery of the Higgs boson. She led a research team for Atlas experiment at CERN and is also responsible for setting up the first masters degree in medical physics in Morocco.

2018

Mexican scientist **CLAUDIA SHEINBAUM** becomes the first woman to be elected to Mayor of Mexico City. Sheinbaum holds a PhD in energy engineering and was jointly awarded the Nobel Peace Prize in 2007 as a member of the Intergovernmental Panel on Climate Change.

3 Third-wave Feminism

1990s onwards

Feminism becomes plural
and intersectional, seeking to
question received notions of
gender and privilege by:
- ending gender violence
- addressing discrimination
- harnessing the power
  of the internet

1989
Fall of
the
Berlin Wall

1992
Maastricht Treaty is
signed, creating the
European Union

2001
9/11
attacks
in New York
and Washington

2003
US invades Iraq in
the first conflict of
the Iraq War

WE SHOULD ALL BE FEMINISTS

Feminist activist Rebecca Walker pointed with fury to the dismissal of Anita Hill's sexual harassment charges in 1992: 'The hearings were not about determining whether or not Clarence Thomas did in fact harass Anita Hill,' she wrote in *Ms.* magazine. 'They were about checking and redefining the extent of women's credibility and power.' Announcing a 'third wave' of feminism, she declared 'the fight is far from over'.

According to Amy Richards, it was the experience 'of having grown up with feminism' that was unique to this generation, who were able to take stock and critique the shortcomings of the previous movement. This meant, in particular, greater inclusivity. In the words of author Chimamanda Ngozi Adichie, 'We should *all* be feminists.' Shaped by Kimberlé Crenshaw's theories of intersectionality, the third wave put an emphasis on making space for the voices of those who had been marginalized – recognizing that class, race, age, ability, sexuality and other issues combine to affect women's experience of gender discrimination. They were wary of homogenizing any assessment of progress.

Ending gender violence was one of their major concerns. The UN Declaration on the Elimination of Violence against Women marked the first framework for

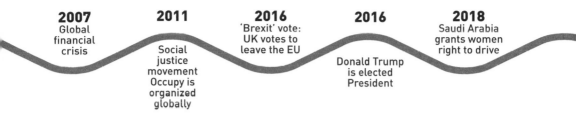

2007
Global
financial
crisis

2011
Social
justice
movement
Occupy is
organized
globally

2016
'Brexit' vote:
UK votes to
leave the EU

2016
Donald Trump
is elected
President

2018
Saudi Arabia
grants women
right to drive

international action of its kind in 1993. Protest movements around the world focused on highlighting destructive attitudes towards sexual assault, from the Denim Day campaign in Italy in 1999 to the first SlutWalk march in Toronto in 2011. From South Africa to Argentina, governments passed legislation to criminalize domestic abuse, while the practice of Female Genital Mutilation was recognized as a human rights violation in seventeen African and eleven industrialised countries from 1994 onwards.

The third wave also meant that for young women there was both the precedent and expectation of female success. Still, despite more than a decade of equal pay legislation, equal pay disputes showed that the workplace remained prejudiced and hostile. In 2017, the World Economic Forum published predictions that it would take another 217 years for disparities in the employment opportunities of men and women to be fully evened out. Working to address the problem, third-wave feminists secured more progressive parental leave legislation with an eye on the 'motherhood penalty'.

Meanwhile, advances in technology reorganized the landscape of feminist discussion: the internet enabled coordination on a fully global scale and the third wave became defined by mass participation. Political breakthroughs in 2018 confirmed the growing empowerment of women around the world, despite the threat posed by the rise of right-wing populism.

| THIRD WAVE IN CONTEXT

Social developments at the end of the twentieth century created new conditions for feminism, which adapted to the digital revolution and climate change anxieties, amongst other changes.

1989 | FALL OF COMMUNISM

On a pitoval evening in European history, East and West Berliners flooded through the borders in their millions and dismantled the Berlin Wall, triggering a movement that saw the collapse of other communist regimes. By 1991, Gorbachev's resignation heralded the dissolution of the USSR. Fifteen states gained independence and over 100 million women won democratic rights.

1991 | DAWN OF THE INTERNET AND THE SOCIAL MEDIA AGE

Set in motion by the launch of the World Wide Web, the digital revolution transformed global communication. In 2004, Mark Zuckerberg founded Facebook: the world's largest social media network with over one billion registered accounts. In 2007, Apple released the first iPhone. These developments proved decisive in the development of third-wave feminism, which harnesses the power of the internet to unite feminists across the globe.

1994 | END OF APARTHEID

The system of institutionalized racial segregation in South Africa known as apartheid was finally repealed in 1991, with fully democratic elections taking place in 1994, which led to the election of the anti-apartheid revolutionary Nelson Mandela. As President, he worked for gender equality, social justice and to end violence against women.

1997 | FIGHTING CLIMATE CHANGE

Mounting anxieties about global warming defined the beginning of the twenty-first century and 192 countries committed to fighting climate change in 1997 by signing the Kyoto Protocol. This was the first international treaty with mandatory aims for the parties who signed it, with specific targets for reducing greenhouse gas emissions.

2000s
RECOGNIZING DIFFERENT GENDER IDENTITIES
This is the decade in which countries started to pass legislation recognizing a change in gender identity, legally affirming that the personal sense of one's gender may or may not correlate with assigned sex at birth. The UK passed legislation in 2004, Spain in 2007, Uruguay in 2009, Argentina in 2012, Denmark in 2014 and Portugal in 2018.

2008
ELECTION OF BARACK OBAMA AND PROGRESSIVE SOCIAL REFORMS
The first African American to be elected to the presidency, Barack Obama was an influential advocate of women's rights throughout his eight-year tenure. He founded the White House Council on Women and Girls in 2009, created a new position, Ambassador-at-Large for Global Women's Issues and introduced the Lilly Ledbetter Fair Pay Act, legislation that tried to address the gender pay gap.

2010
FIGHTING FOR DEMOCRACY IN THE ARAB SPRING
The series of uprisings known as the Arab Spring began in Tunisia in protest at the authoritarian regime.The unrest soon spread to Libya, Egypt, Yemen, Syria and Bahrain and the movement saw a significant expansion in women's political participation. With several new governments installed in its aftermath, many hoped the Spring would lead to improvements in women's rights. However, the results did not match expectations.

2016
RISE OF RIGHT-WING POPULISM
Internationally, politics saw a rise in right-wing populism at the expense of progressive politics, posing a threat to both women's rights and democracy in general. In the biggest blow to social equality movements, Donald Trump, who advocated for an abortion ban and pledged in his campaign to repeal Obamacare, was elected President in the US in 2016.

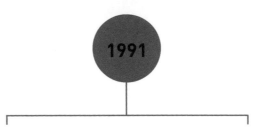

1991

US

ANITA HILL FILES A SEXUAL HARASSMENT CASE AGAINST CLARENCE THOMAS, A NOMINEE FOR THE SUPREME COURT. HER TESTIMONY IS BROADCAST ON TELEVISION AND MANY ARE INCENSED AT HER INSENSITIVE, BIAS-RIDDLED HEARING BY AN ALL-MALE PANEL. REBECCA WALKER'S RESPONSE IN *MS.* MAGAZINE IS A CALL TO ARMS: 'THE FIGHT IS FAR FROM OVER … I AM THE THIRD WAVE'.

LET THIS DISMISSAL OF A WOMAN'S EXPERIENCE MOVE YOU TO ANGER. TURN THAT OUTRAGE INTO POLITICAL POWER.

REBECCA WALKER (1969–)

THE DAUGHTER OF WRITER ALICE WALKER
AND INTERNATIONALLY FAMOUS WRITER
AND ACTIVIST

'The issue of sexual harassment is not the end of it. There are other issues – political issues, gender issues – that people need to be educated about.'

Law professor Anita Hill is remembered for her bold testimony against Supreme Court nominee Clarence Thomas in 1991. Appearing before an all-male, white panel, Hill brought the issue of sexual harassment to public prominence, speaking out about Thomas' advances and explicit remarks in televised hearings that were watched by millions. The Senate approved Thomas' nomination, but the case provoked widespread debate about gender relations in the workplace. As an attorney and academic, Hill continued to be an outspoken advocate of women's rights and civil rights throughout her career. In 1997 she published her autobiography *Speaking Truth to Power*. In 2017 she was selected to lead the Commission on Sexual Harassment and Advancing Equality in the Workplace. In 2018, her story resonated through a parallel case, when Dr Christine Blasey Ford accused Supreme Court nominee Brett Kavanaugh of sexual assault. He was likewise confirmed.

Anita Hill
AMERICAN

1956–

ANITA
HILL

THIRD-WAVE FEMINIST THEORY

As one of several influential developments in feminist theory, the concept of intersectionality is part of what defines the third wave. Feminists became more self-conscious about the ways in which women may experience oppression in varying configurations and in varying degrees of intensity.

1989

African-American professor **KIMBERLÉ CRENSHAW** coins 'intersectionality' in her paper 'Demarginalizing the Intersection of Race and Sex'. Her academic term is now at the forefront of feminist conversations and used more broadly to explain how gender, race, class, ability and sexual orientation intersect to affect women's experiences of oppression across the world, as well as to make space for the issues of those women who have been marginalized.

African-American writer and poet **AUDRE LORDE** publishes *Sister Outsider*, a collection of essays and speeches that tackles the intersection of sexism, homophobia, racism, classism and ageism.

1990

African-American professor **PATRICIA COLLINS** publishes *Black Feminist Thought*, which studies the specific experience of black women in the context of intersectional feminism.

American philosopher **JUDITH BUTLER** publishes *Gender Trouble: Feminism and the Subversion of Identity*. In this highly influential book, Butler throws into question the idea of a universal concept of 'womanhood', arguing that gender, sex and sexuality are social constructions.

1991
American journalist **NAOMI WOLF** publishes *The Beauty Myth* in which she argues that beauty is a social construct that negatively impacts women in five areas: work, religion, sex, violence and hunger.

1991
Indian professor **CHANDRA TALPADE MOHANTY** publishes 'Under Western Eyes', an article that criticizes the exclusion of women from the Global South from feminist theory.

1993
Australian philosopher **VAL PLUMWOOD** publishes *Feminism and the Mastery of Nature*, which considers the parallels between the domination of nature and the domination of women. Both standpoints, she argues, originate from a set of views that sees 'the other as radically separate and inferior ... derivative or peripheral to that of the self or centre, and whose agency is denied or minimalized'.

2014
Japanese feminist **EMI KOYAMA** publishes *The Transfeminist Manifesto*. Emi defines transfeminism as 'a movement by and for trans women who view their liberation to be intrinsically linked to the liberation of all women and beyond'.

American writer **REBECCA SOLNIT** publishes her essay collection *Men Explain Things to Me* in which she discusses the silencing of women according to men's assumption that men always know better or know more. This phenomenon is now known as 'mansplaining'.

2017
British professor **MARY BEARD** publishes *Women and Power*, an analysis of female silence from Roman antiquity which shows that 'power' has historically been understood according to a male template.

2018
JACQUELINE ROSE publishes *Mothers: An Essay on Love and Cruelty*, which examines the ways in which mothers are held accountable for the world's ills and made the objects of 'licensed cruelty', combining insights from investigative writing, psychoanalysis, social history and literature.

1999

ITALY

THE FIRST DENIM DAY PROTEST, SPARKED BY WIDESPREAD OUTCRY AT ITALY'S SUPREME COURT RULING THAT THE VICTIM CAN'T HAVE BEEN RAPED BECAUSE SHE WAS WEARING TIGHT JEANS.

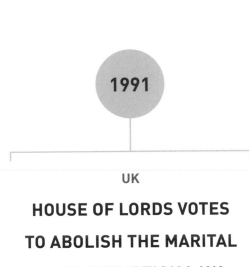

1991

UK

HOUSE OF LORDS VOTES TO ABOLISH THE MARITAL RAPE EXEMPTION LAW, MEANING HUSBANDS CAN BE CONVICTED OF RAPE.

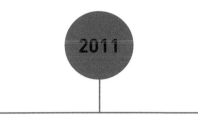

2011

3,000 GATHER IN TORONTO CALLING FOR AN END TO RAPE CULTURE, PROMPTED BY A POLICE OFFICER'S COMMENT 'WOMEN SHOULD AVOID DRESSING LIKE SLUTS' TO PRECAUTION AGAINST HARASSMENT. THE MOVEMENT BECOMES INTERNATIONAL, WITH RALLIES IN MORE THAN SEVEN COUNTRIES.

2016

ARGENTINA

THE GRASSROOTS FEMINIST COLLECTIVE *NI UNA MENOS* ('NOT ONE WOMAN LESS') ORGANIZES A MASS WOMEN'S STRIKE IN RESPONSE TO THE RAPE AND MURDER OF LUCIA PEREZ. THIS PROTEST AGAINST FEMICIDE AND *MACHISTA* VIOLENCE SPREADS TO CHILE, PERU, BOLIVIA, GUATEMALA, URUGUAY, MEXICO, SPAIN AND BEYOND.

'I raise up my voice – not so I can shout, but so that those without a voice can be heard.'

Pakistani activist Malala Yousafzai has been an activist since 2009 when she stood up for girls' right to an education in her native Swat Valley. Aged eleven, Malala blogged about her experiences under the Taliban in an anonymous diary for the BBC, lamenting the closure of girls' schools in Swat. As the schools reopened and her diary ended, Malala continued to campaign for girls' education in speeches on television and radio, leading to her nomination for the International Children's Peace Prize in 2011. In 2012 she was shot by the Taliban on her way home from school, prompting a wave of global support for Malala and her cause. Following her recovery, she established the Malala Fund, a charity dedicated to giving every girl the opportunity to determine her future. In recognition of her charity work and activism, Malala was awarded the Nobel Peace Prize in 2014, becoming its youngest ever recipient.

Malala Yousafzai

PAKISTANI

1997–

MALALA YOUSAFZAI

2013

CHINA

FIRST WOMAN TO BRING A
GENDER DISCRIMINATION
LAWSUIT IN CHINA WINS A
SMALL SETTLEMENT. THE
PRIVATE TUTORING FIRM,
JUREN ACADEMY, REFUSED
TO GIVE CAO JU
AN ASSISTANT POST
BECAUSE SHE
WAS A WOMAN.

2015

GERMANY

PARLIAMENT PASSES
LEGISLATION TO INTRODUCE
A *FRAUENQUOTE* OR
'WOMEN'S QUOTA'.
CORPORATE BOARDS OF
LARGE COMPANIES ARE
REQUIRED TO BE AT LEAST
30 PER CENT FEMALE.

2018

2018

UK AND US

ICELAND

INSTITUTE FOR FISCAL
STUDIES AND PRINCETON
UNIVERSITY SUGGEST
THE GENDER PAY GAP IS
CAUSED BY A 'MOTHERHOOD
PENALTY': EXPERIENCING
A SHARP DECLINE IN
EARNINGS AFTER THE BIRTH
OF THEIR FIRST CHILD,
MOTHERS EARN
20 PER CENT LESS THAN
MALE COUNTERPARTS
OVER THE COURSE
OF THEIR CAREER.

RANKING BEST IN
THE WORLD IN TERMS
OF GENDER PAY GAP FOR
THE EIGHTH YEAR IN A
ROW, THE GOVERNMENT
PASSES LEGISLATION
PLEDGING TO ELIMINATE
THE GENDER PAY GAP BY
2022. ICELAND BECOMES THE
FIRST COUNTRY TO FORCE
COMPANIES TO PROVE THEY
PAY EVERYONE EQUALLY.

| WOMEN IN ART

Women have always animated the world of visual arts, but more women started to be seen and appreciated as visual artists from the 1960s onwards; below is a selection of artists who have used their talent to contribute to the women's movement and to the fight for equal rights.

1938

Mexican artist **FRIDA KAHLO** secures her first solo exhibition at Julien Levy's gallery in Manhattan. Her art is strongly autobiographical and her persona is inspired by Mexican folk culture and matriarchy. Known until the 70s for her marriage to artist Diego Rivera, she is later rediscovered for her own art and its strongly feminist value.

1964

Japanese-American conceptual artist **YOKO ONO** stages her 'Cut Piece', a feminist performance in which she invites the audience to use scissors to cut her clothes off her, symbolizing the objectification of women. She is one of the strongest feminist voices in the art world in the 60s.

1967

American photographer **DIANE ARBUS'** work is included in an exhibition at the Museum of Modern Art in New York. Her subjects are often outsiders fighting with their identity as well as the depiction of ordinary life and its disquieting feel. In 1972, she becomes the first photographer whose work was included in the selection of Venice Biennale. She had committed suicide the year before.

1970

French visual artist and sculptor **LOUISE BOURGEOIS** organizes her 'bloody Sundays', a cycle of art critique sessions where she challenges her fellow artists' real involvement with feminism. She is among the first to use images of the female body to comment on gender stereotypes.

1985

North American collective **GUERILLA GIRLS** is founded in New York. Their performances and graphic art focus on the lack of representation of women and minority groups in art museums and galleries and a criticism of stereotypes in Hollywood and popular culture.

1998

British visual artist **TRACEY EMIN** creates her *My Bed* installation using personal narrative and objects to comment on femininity and gender.

1999

Guatemalan poet and visual artist **REGINA JOSÉ GALINDO** protests against the silencing of women's voices by suspending herself from the post office arch in Guatemala's capital and reading her poetry.

2009

Mexican artist **ELINA CHAUVET** creates her first *Zapatos Rojos* ('Red Shoes') installation to protest against violence against women killed by drug smugglers. From that moment the red shoes become the symbol of the International Day Against Violence Against Women.

2011

Russian feminist punk rock band **PUSSY RIOT** stages unauthorised guerrilla performances in public places on feminist and LGBT issues and state their opposition to President Vladimir Putin.

2015

Portuguese artist **JOANA VASCONCELOS** shows her work *A noiva* ('The Bride'), a chandelier made of over 25,000 tampons, at Venice Biennale. She is the first woman and youngest contemporary artist to exhibit in Versailles.

2017

Japanese visual artist **YAYOI KUSAMA** has a museum named in her honour in Tokyo. Born in 1929, she began her career in the early 1960s, using her body as a canvas, covered in red polka dots, to champion sexual liberation. She provided a precursor to the feminist performance art movement.

'I have chosen to no longer be apologetic for my femaleness and my femininity.'

In 2012, award-winning fiction writer Chimamanda Ngozi Adichie delivered the TEDxTalk that would fuel an international debate about feminism's meaning in the 21st century. Its title was 'We Should All Be Feminists'. In it she argued powerfully and plainly for a positive, inclusive definition of the term. Viewed more than five million times, the lecture was published as a book-length essay in 32 languages; in Sweden, the Women's Lobby announced an initiative to gift the book to every 16-year-old in the country's school system. Adichie's fiction has won numerous awards, including the Orange Prize, and she is also the author of *Dear Ijeawele, or a Feminist Manifesto in Fifteen Suggestions* (2017), which takes the form of advice to her daughter, urging her to find strength and pride as an independent woman.

Chimamanda Ngozi Adichie
NIGERIAN

1977–

CHIMAMANDA
NGOZI ADICHIE

| PARENTAL LEAVE POLICIES AROUND THE WORLD

Parental leave has been an important tool in promoting gender equality, enabling mothers and fathers to share the responsibility of childrearing. According to the International Labour Organization 178 out of 196 countries around the world guarantee paid leave for working mothers, while more than 50 countries provide paternity benefits.

	SWEDEN	DENMARK*	PORTUGAL	FINLAND	NORWAY	FRANCE	SWITZERLAND	AUSTRIA	NETHERLANDS	CANADA	GERMANY*	BELGIUM	UNITED KINGDOM*	SPAIN
WOMEN'S LABOUR FORCE PARTICIPATION (As a percentage)	84.9	84.4	84.4	83.8	83.4	82.8	82.3	82.3	82.3	81.3	81.3	80.4	78.7	78.3
COST OF CHILDCARE (As a percent of net family income)	4.7	8.9	4.8	8.4	10.8	10.4	50.6	11.8	10.1	18.5	11.1	4.7	26.6	4.7
PAID PATERNITY LEAVE?	✓	✓	✓	✓	✓	✓	✗	✗	✓	✗	✗	✓	✓	✓
LENGTH OF PAID MATERNITY LEAVE (In weeks)	16	18	17/21	18	35/45	16	14	16	16	17	14	15	39	16
PERCENT OF WAGES (During maternity leave)		100		70		100 †	80 †	100	100 †		100			100

80% for the first 390 days, then flat rate

100% (or 80% for 150 days)

100% (or 80% for 45 weeks)

55% for 15 weeks up to a ceiling

82% for the first 30 days; 75% for the remainder (up to a ceiling)

6 weeks paid at 90%; lower of 90% or flat rate for weeks 7-39

Key

-  Europe
- Asia
- N. America
- Australasia
- Africa
- † Up to a ceiling
- *Optional additional parental leave benefits

	AUSTRALIA*	NEW ZEALAND	UNITED STATES*	GHANA	ICELAND	GREECE	IRELAND	ITALY	JAPAN*	CHINA	SINGAPORE	RUSSIA	LITHUANIA	ALBANIA	SERBIA*	INDIA	IRAQ
	75.2	76.9	75.2	75	73	72.2	72.2	71.6	64.4	61	60	57	56	47	46	27	19
	14.5	19.6	23.1			3.2	25.6		16.9								
	✓	✓	✗	✗	✓	✓	✗	✓	✗	✓	✓	✗	✓	✗	✓	✗	✓
	52	14	0	12	39	17	42	22	14	14	16	20	18	52	20	26	9
		100 †	0	1	80	100		90	67		100	100	100		100	100	100

80% for the first 6 months, then 50%

Allowance based on average salary of company's employes

80% up to a ceiling for 26 weeks

18 weeks at the federal minimum level

2018

2018

SPAIN

OVER FIVE MILLION WORKERS TAKE PART IN SPAIN'S FIRST FEMINIST STRIKE ON INTERNATIONAL WOMEN'S DAY TO DRAW ATTENTION TO SPAIN'S MISOGYNISTIC CULTURE. THE SLOGAN OF THE DAY WAS 'IF WE STOP, THE WORLD STOPS'.

UK

CARRIE GRACIE WINS HER EQUAL PAY DISPUTE AGAINST THE BBC. ONE OF THE BBC'S MOST SENIOR JOURNALISTS, SHE HAD RESIGNED FROM HER POST AFTER IT WAS REVEALED SHE WAS PAID UP TO £100,000 LESS THAN HER MALE PEERS. SHE DONATES THE £280,000 SETTLEMENT TO THE FAWCETT SOCIETY.

"

IF YOU TELL ME I'M
RUBBISH, I MIGHT
BELIEVE YOU, BUT
IF YOU TELL ME SHE'S
RUBBISH I KNOW
IT'S NOT TRUE.

CARRIE GRACIE (1962–)
SCOTTISH JOURNALIST AND FORMER
CHINA EDITOR FOR THE BBC

| WOMEN'S MARCH 2017

On 21 January, more than seven million people stage marches in more than 80 countries in protest at the threat posed to women's rights by President Trump's administration.

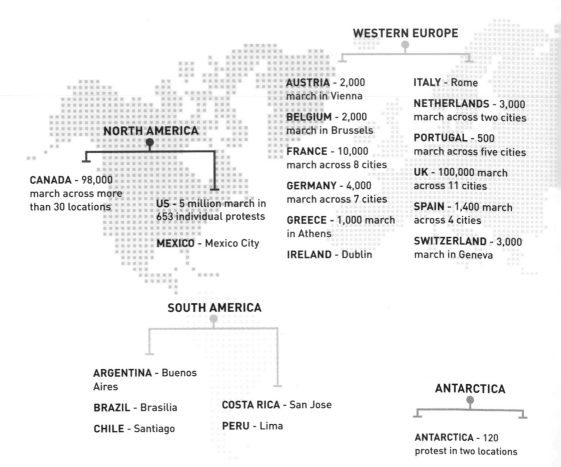

WESTERN EUROPE

NORTH AMERICA

CANADA - 98,000 march across more than 30 locations

US - 5 million march in 653 individual protests

MEXICO - Mexico City

AUSTRIA - 2,000 march in Vienna

BELGIUM - 2,000 march in Brussels

FRANCE - 10,000 march across 8 cities

GERMANY - 4,000 march across 7 cities

GREECE - 1,000 march in Athens

IRELAND - Dublin

ITALY - Rome

NETHERLANDS - 3,000 march across two cities

PORTUGAL - 500 march across five cities

UK - 100,000 march across 11 cities

SPAIN - 1,400 march across 4 cities

SWITZERLAND - 3,000 march in Geneva

SOUTH AMERICA

ARGENTINA - Buenos Aires

BRAZIL - Brasilia

CHILE - Santiago

COSTA RICA - San Jose

PERU - Lima

ANTARCTICA

ANTARCTICA - 120 protest in two locations

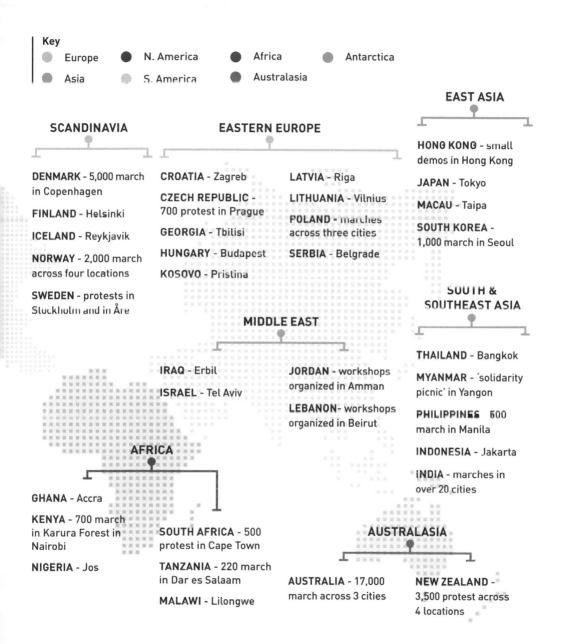

Key
- Europe
- Asia
- N. America
- S. America
- Africa
- Australasia
- Antarctica

EAST ASIA

HONG KONG - small demos in Hong Kong

JAPAN - Tokyo

MACAU - Taipa

SOUTH KOREA - 1,000 march in Seoul

SCANDINAVIA

DENMARK - 5,000 march in Copenhagen

FINLAND - Helsinki

ICELAND - Reykjavik

NORWAY - 2,000 march across four locations

SWEDEN - protests in Stockholm and in Åre

EASTERN EUROPE

CROATIA - Zagreb

CZECH REPUBLIC - 700 protest in Prague

GEORGIA - Tbilisi

HUNGARY - Budapest

KOSOVO - Pristina

LATVIA - Riga

LITHUANIA - Vilnius

POLAND - marches across three cities

SERBIA - Belgrade

MIDDLE EAST

IRAQ - Erbil

ISRAEL - Tel Aviv

JORDAN - workshops organized in Amman

LEBANON - workshops organized in Beirut

SOUTH & SOUTHEAST ASIA

THAILAND - Bangkok

MYANMAR - 'solidarity picnic' in Yangon

PHILIPPINES 500 march in Manila

INDONESIA - Jakarta

INDIA - marches in over 20 cities

AFRICA

GHANA - Accra

KENYA - 700 march in Karura Forest in Nairobi

NIGERIA - Jos

SOUTH AFRICA - 500 protest in Cape Town

TANZANIA - 220 march in Dar es Salaam

MALAWI - Lilongwe

AUSTRALASIA

AUSTRALIA - 17,000 march across 3 cities

NEW ZEALAND - 3,500 protest across 4 locations

111

WOMEN IN SPORT

Sport has been one of the toughest areas in which women have overcome gender discrimination. Still, female participation in sport has risen dramatically in the past century. The athletes below have set precedents and provided global inspiration.

1926

Record-breaking American swimmer **GERTRUDE EDERLE** makes history when she becomes the first woman to swim the English Channel.

1932

American aviator and author **AMELIA EARHART** is the first woman to fly solo across the Atlantic Ocean. An advocate of equal rights, she is essential in the formation of the Ninety-Nines, an organization for female pilots. She is an early supporter of the Equal Rights Amendment.

1958

Italian **MARIA TERSA DE FILIPPIS** becomes the first woman to compete in a Formula One race at the Belgian Grand Prix. She goes on to participate in two more Grands Prix in Italy and Portugal.

1964

Soviet gymnast **LARISSA LATYNINA** completes her Olympic career with a total of 18 medals - more than any other athlete in Olympic history.

1973

World number one tennis player **BILLIE JEAN KING** defeats Bobby Riggs in the 'Battle of the Sexes' tennis match. An advocate of gender equality, she founds the Women's Tennis Association and the Women's Sport Foundation.

1975

Japanese mountaineer **JUNKO TABEI,** founder of the Ladies Climbing Club, becomes the first woman to climb Mount Everest. During the ascent, an avalanche strikes the camp and Tabei reportedly loses consciousness for six minutes under the snow until her guide digs her out. She went on to summit the highest peaks in more than 70 countries.

1986

American **NANCY LIEBERMAN** becomes the first woman to play in a professional men's basketball league. She is also the first woman to coach a professional men's team as the head coach of the Texas Legends in the NBA Developmental League in 2009.

1994

Czech-American tennis player **MARTINA NAVRATILOVA** retires with an all-time male or female record of 1,438 match wins to her credit.

1994

ANN DANIELS and **CAROLINE HAMILTON** become the first women to trek to both the South Pole and the North Pole as part of an all-women team.

2005

British sailor **ELLEN MACARTHUR** breaks the world record for the fastest solo navigation of the world, sailing 27,354 nautical miles in 71 days.

2015

ENI ALUKO is named player of the year by the Chelsea Football Club and player of the match in the FA Cup Final. She has made 102 appearances for England and also holds a first class honours degree in Law.

1993

UK

HAVING BEEN EFFECTIVELY BANNED BY THE FOOTBALL ASSOCIATION (FA) IN 1921, WOMEN'S FOOTBALL IS BROUGHT UNDER THE CONTROL OF THIS NATIONAL GOVERNING BODY IN A MAJOR RECOGNITION OF THE SPORT. THE FA CREATES THE WOMEN'S FA CHALLENGE CUP THAT YEAR AND 137 TEAMS ENTER.

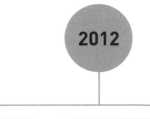

2012

QATAR, SAUDI ARABIA, BRUNEI

WOMEN ATHLETES FROM SAUDI ARABIA, QATAR AND BRUNEI COMPETE IN THE OLYMPICS FOR THE FIRST TIME.

"

THE SUCCESS OF EVERY WOMAN SHOULD BE THE INSPIRATION TO ANOTHER. WE SHOULD RAISE EACH OTHER UP.

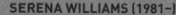

SERENA WILLIAMS (1981–)

AMERICAN TENNIS CHAMPION WHOSE SINGLES GRAND SLAM RECORD RANKS THE BEST IN TENNIS HISTORY

US

1992

THE CENTRE FOR REPRODUCTIVE RIGHTS IS ESTABLISHED, A LEGAL ADVOCACY ORGANIZATION THAT SAFEGUARDS WOMEN'S REPRODUCTIVE RIGHTS WORLDWIDE. THEIR ATTORNEYS HAVE SINCE STRENGTHENED LAWS AND POLICIES IN MORE THAN 50 COUNTRIES

ZIMBABWE

1993

CAMPAIGN FOR FEMALE EDUCATION (CAMFED) IS FOUNDED TO ENABLE A GROUP OF 32 GIRLS TO ATTEND SECONDARY SCHOOL. BY 2018, SUPPORT HAD BEEN EXTENDED TO MORE THAN 2.6 MILLION CHILDREN THROUGH A NETWORK OF MORE THAN 5,000 SCHOOLS THROUGHOUT SOUTHERN AFRICA

2008

US

THE INDEPENDENT NON-
PROFIT 'GIRL EFFECT' IS
LAUNCHED. ITS WORK IS
BASED ON THE BELIEF
THAT, WHEN GIVEN THE
OPPORTUNITY, GIRLS
ARE ABLE TO LIFT THEIR
COUNTRIES OUT OF POVERTY.
CREATED BY THE NIKE
FOUNDATION, THE CHARITY
NOW WORKS FROM NINE
GLOBAL LOCATIONS AND IS
ACTIVE IN 66 COUNTRIES.

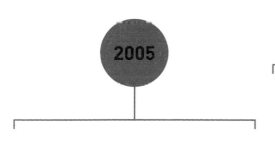

2005

US

THE GLOBAL FUND FOR
WOMEN SETS UP THE
LEGACY FUND, THE LARGEST
ENDOWMENT IN THE WORLD
DEDICATED EXCLUSIVELY
TO WOMEN'S RIGHTS.
THIS FUND PROVIDES
$8 MILLION A YEAR TO
WOMEN-LED ORGANIZATIONS.

'The measure of any society is how it treats its women and girls.'

Lawyer and former First Lady Michelle Obama has been a powerful and outspoken champion of women's rights throughout her career. In her role as the first African American to serve as First Lady, she helped to shape the most inclusive White House in history and launched the priority initiative Let Girls Learn. The programme invests in girls' education projects to empower and offer opportunities to the 62 million girls who are currently not in school. She has also been an influential advocate for poverty awareness, healthy eating and the initiatives of Obama's presidency, including the Lilly Ledbetter Fair Pay Act of 2009. An Ivy League graduate, she met the 44th US President as his mentor at a Chicago law firm. Her inspiring story was published in her memoir *Becoming* in 2018. It details her experiences of balancing the demands of motherhood with one of the world's most high-profile, unofficial jobs.

Michelle Obama

AMERICAN

1964–

MICHELLE
OBAMA

2009

BOLIVIA

BOLIVIA PASSES A CONSTITUTIONAL AMENDMENT THAT REQUIRES EQUAL GENDER LEGISLATION IN GOVERNMENT. AS OF 2017, THE LEGISLATURE IS 53 PER CENT WOMEN AND RANKS SECOND IN THE WORLD.

2017

RWANDA

RWANDA RECEIVES INTERNATIONAL RECOGNITION FOR BEST FEMALE REPRESENTATION IN GOVERNMENT: 61 PER CENT OF MPS ARE WOMEN, THE HIGHEST PROPORTION IN THE WORLD.

2018

US

WOMEN CANDIDATES MAKE
HISTORY IN THE MIDTERM
ELECTIONS WITH A RECORD-
BREAKING 90 WOMEN
ELECTED TO THE HOUSE
OF REPRESENTATIVES.
RASHIDA TLAIB AND ILHAM
OMAR BECOME THE FIRST
MUSLIM WOMEN ELECTED TO
CONGRESS, DEB HAALAND
AND SHARICE DAVIDS
THE FIRST NATIVE
AMERICAN WOMEN.

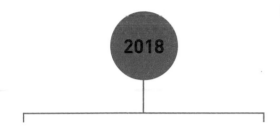

2018

US

GLOBAL FUND FOR WOMEN
HELPS TO CHANGE
18 LAWS IN 14 COUNTRIES
THROUGHOUT THE
YEAR, INCLUDING THE
LEGALIZATION OF
ABORTION IN CHILE.

| WOMEN IN SOCIAL MEDIA

In the twenty-first century, social media has revolutionized how feminists organize, with new global platforms for establishing communities, sharing experiences and gathering support to guarantee change. Below we showcase notable social media feminists and how they have harnessed the power of the internet.

2009
Canadian American **ANITA SARKEESIAN** begins the vlog feministfrequency.com to heighten awareness of sexist tropes in popular culture and make the media more feminist. The YouTube channel attracts over 200,000 subscribers and partners with Intel in 2015 to increase diversity and inclusivity in the technology industry.

2012
LAURA BATES founds the Everyday Sexism project in the UK, a platform for women to share their experiences of day-to-day gender inequality. Within 20 months, the project has a global presence with 50,000 entries and has expanded to 18 countries, documenting all experiences of sexism from the minor to the catastrophic.

2013
In Germany, **ANNE WIZOREK** starts #aufschrei ('outcry'), which goes viral as women share their experiences of sexual harassment following sexist remarks by FDP politician Rainer Brüderle.

2014
Footage showing NFL player Ray Rice beating his then-fiancée Janay Rice sparks a public conversation about domestic abuse, in response to which American writer **BEVERLY GOODEN** launches the #WhyIStayed campaign to highlight the complexities of leaving an abusive relationship.

2014 Brit **LAURA CORYTON** starts the online petition 'Stop Taxing Periods. Period.', which successfully pressures the UK government into ending 'tampon tax' and continues to support global sister campaigns.

2015 Afghan **LALEH OSMANI** creates #whereismyname to challenge people to use women's names in defiance of Afghan cultural taboos.

2016 In Poland, **MAŁGORZATA ADAMCZYK** initiates the hashtag campaign #czarnyprotest ('black protest') in which people share selfies wearing black to protest against tighter abortion laws. The hashtag was to become the most shared Polish hashtag of the year, reaching 44.5 million people.

2017 The #PropertyForHer campaign is launched on social media in South Asia by **KAMLA BHASIN**. The campaign asks parents to pledge to leave their daughter an equal share of property, and asks brothers to stand by their sisters: 'Your daughter in your heart and in your will'.

2017 American actress **ALYSSA MILANO** encourages women around the world to share their experiences of sexual violence using **TARANA BURKE**'s hashtag #MeToo. The campaign gains huge global momentum publicizing the prevalence of rape and sexual assault. On Facebook, the hashtag is used by more than 4.7 million users in the first 24 hours. Sister hashtags spread to more than 85 countries: in Spain it becomes #YoTambien, in France #BalanceTonPorc ('expose your pig') and in Italy #quellavoltache ('that time when').

FEMINISM NOW: THE 'FOURTH WAVE'

Each generation of feminists reshapes the goals and priorities of the women's movement. The twenty-first century is no different. Feminism continues to evolve in today's internationally minded, digitally driven environment. Labelling this recent surge the 'fourth wave', some argue that social media has fundamentally changed the face of feminism. Online platforms have mobilized younger generations, enabled the movement's increasing breadth and emboldened women to speak out about the everyday instances of sexism they encounter, both in person and in the media.

What has not changed are the reasons to call yourself a feminist. At the level of society and politics, in our attitudes and in our actions, inequality persists. On the basis of gender, women and men are regarded and treated differently. Feminism will continue to demand your conviction and commitment until women across the world can speak freely and live without fear.

This book has shone a light onto what can be achieved when we stand together, speak out together and refuse to back down. But feminism begins with individuals: this book should show you that feminism also starts with you. If you can highlight the changes that still have to happen, if you can call out the sexism or inequalities you encounter, you can make a difference.

With courage, with determination, with hope, the future is female.

WOMEN FEATURED

RESOURCES

This book has provided a snapshot of the history of feminism. If you would like to find out more about the history and achievements of the women's movement, start by exploring the collections of the libraries below.

AUSTRALIA

Jessie Street National Women's Library
www.nationalwomenslibrary.org.au
Ultimo Community Centre
523-525 Harris Street
Ultimo NSW 2007
Sydney

The Women's Library
thewomenslibrary.org.au
8-10 Brown St
Newtown NSW 2040

NEW ZEALAND

Auckland Woman's Centre
awc.orq.nz
4 Warnock Street
Grey Lynn
Auckland 1021

UK

Feminist Library
feministlibrary.co.uk
5 Westminster Bridge Road
London SE1 7XW

Women's Library, London
www.lse.ac.uk/library/collections
Formerly the Fawcett Library
LSE, Houghton Street
London WC2A 2AE

Pankhurst Centre, Manchester
www.pankhursttrust.org
60-62 Nelson St
Manchester M13 9WP

Feminist Archive North, Leeds
feministarchivenorth.org.uk
University of Leeds
Brotherton Library
Woodhouse Ln
Leeds LS2 9JT

Feminist Archive South, Bristol
feministarchivesouth.org.uk
University of Bristol
Beacon House
Queens Road
Bristol BS8 1QU

Glasgow Women's Library
womenslibrary.org.uk
23 Landressy St
Glasgow G40 1BP

Swansea Women's Centre
www.womensarchivewales.org
25 Mansel Street
Swansea SA1 5SQ

First published in Great Britain, Australia and New Zealand in 2019 by
Modern Books
An imprint of Elwin Street Productions Limited
14 Clerkenwell Green
London EC1R 0DP
www.modern-books.com

Illustrations by Rebecca Strickson © (cover, 8, 48, 84, 125)
Internal design by Natalie Clay
Additional text by Jessica Payn

Additional picture credits:
Alamy Stock Photo: © dpa picture alliance, 104; © Everett Collection Historical, 59; © Everett Collection Inc, 71; © Granger Historical Picture Archive, 31; © INTERFOTO, 67; © Keystone Pictures USA, 62; © Kristoffer Tripplaar, 119; © Paul Pickard, 99; © Photo 12/Archives Snark, 37; © SCPhotos, 92; © World History Archive, 19. © Shutterstock, 26–27, 38–39, 64–65, 76–77, 80–81, 110–111.

978-1-912-82710-7

10 9 8 7 6 5 4 3 2 1

Printed in Slovenia